The Bigamist

The Bigamist

The True Story of a Husband's Ultimate Betrayal

Mary Turner Thomson

Little
a

Previously published in 2008 by Mainstream Publishing.

Published by Little A, Seattle

www.apub.com

Amazon, the Amazon logo, and Little A are trademarks of Amazon.com, Inc.,
or its affiliates.

ISBN-13: 9781542024969
ISBN-10: 154202496X

Cover design by The Brewster Project

Printed in the United States of America

For my wonderful mum,
who taught me truth, integrity and respect,
who gave me strength and courage
and who told me to write this down

AUTHOR'S NOTE

This is the true story and as genuine an account as I can produce of what happened to me. With hindsight, it is possible to see some of what was real and what was not – but this book is written from the perspective of what I knew to be the truth at the time, and why I believed it.

Too many people are abused by lies and deceit. I have yet to meet anyone who has never been conned, deceived or lied to at some point in their lives. People who discover their partner's affairs feel ashamed and belittled, as if somehow they should have known, particularly if others around them suspected earlier than they did. There is a perception of idiocy when a person has been deceived by someone they love and trust, though in fact to trust people, and particularly your lover, is completely natural. Those of us who have been deceived are made to feel stupid and embarrassed, although we have done nothing but have faith in someone who professed love.

To protect those who do not want to be recognised, I have changed all the names in this book except for my own and that of Will Jordan. I was often asked if I would write it under a pseudonym, as it was thought that I might not want people to know who I am. The question itself betrays a social perception I want to change. Why should people feel ashamed or humiliated because they have been the victim of a crime? I am not proud of what has happened but I certainly do not feel the need to hide it. It's that very perception that keeps so many people trapped in silence and unable to talk about their own abusive situation. If this book can help others who have been through something similar, then all the better.

I had initially hoped to include excerpts from the original emails and messages that I received and kept from Will Jordan, in order to tell the story in both the words of the prey and the predator. Unfortunately, however, these have been removed due to legal advice, but I have been careful to convey the tone of Will's correspondence accurately and without exaggeration from the originals.

This book is for my three wonderful children – Robyn, Eilidh and Zach: they are my salvation, my heart and soul, and deserved better than the hand they were dealt. They had to grow up without a father and without any paternal child support or financial investment in their future. They have come to terms with what happened to us all and this book helped them to understand without bitterness or regret.

When this book was originally published in 2007, my children were only eight, five and two years old – so I changed their names. At the time of publishing this third edition they are now twenty-one, eighteen and fifteen years old. Now older, they have specifically asked me to use their real names, so I have.

PROLOGUE

5 April 2006

It was a Wednesday morning – a damp, grey April day – and my three young children were starting to play up. They needed to get out of the house, so I decided on a trip to the library to get some fresh air and some new picture books to entertain them. While trying to get them ready, one shoe remained elusive and I was spending more time looking for it than should have been necessary. I was grateful for the distraction, however, and was keeping myself active, as it meant I didn't have to think about everything else that was going on.

The phone rang and I answered with a quick, distracted, 'Hello.'

'Are you Mary Turner Thomson?' asked a woman's voice.

'Yes,' I replied with some trepidation. I was dreading a phone call from my husband's female lawyer that would tell me how his court case had gone that morning. If it was her voice on the other end of the line, it meant that he was in jail, having been found guilty of trumped-up charges of bigamy, fraud, firearms offences and not registering his address under the Sexual Offences Act.

I knew none of it was true. Will had explained everything to me. I had known for some time now that he was a CIA agent and that the problems had arisen when he'd tried to get out of the service. He had been set up. The marriage certificate the police were using as evidence against him was part of a cover story set up by his employers to explain his presence in the country; the firearms charges and failure to register as a sex offender were also related to his work; and the fraud charges had arisen due to a misunderstanding. Will had warned me that powerful forces were working against him and he expected to receive a short jail sentence. But he assured me that once he was out, it would all be over. He would be free and we would be together finally as a family.

This call snapped me back to the nightmare, but I could not have imagined what was going to come next.

'Are you also Mrs Jordan?' the voice asked.

'Yes,' I said again, now feeling a building knot of anxiety.

'I am the other Mrs Jordan,' she said and, without pause and before I could react in any way, delivered the second punch. 'Have you been told I am an agent?'

Stunned and still reeling, I automatically replied, 'Yes.'

'I was told *you* were an agent,' she said.

The blood ran hot through my veins, flooding my whole body with warmth. It rushed to my brain and I felt myself start to shake. I have never experienced a reaction like it and it was totally physical, not emotional. I had no emotion at that moment in time; I was numb in the truest sense of the word. Nothing I had ever felt was real, nothing I knew was real; everything was gone.

The facade of my life crumbled around me. I knew she was telling the truth. I had probably known for some time but had just refused to believe it, refused to give up on hope and accept that my bizarre life was a sham. Now hope was gone, there was nothing left, and deep down I had known all along it was coming.

For more than an hour, I listened to Michelle as she pulled my life apart with her truth. She calmly told me that she and my

2

husband Will Jordan, the father of my two younger children, had been married for fourteen years and had five children together.

He'd had numerous affairs and had fathered two children with Michelle's nanny. In fact, as she talked I realised that all three of us, Michelle, her nanny and I, had four-year-olds with the same father. It was more than likely that we had all been pregnant at the same time; in fact, they had both been pregnant when Will first contacted me.

Michelle sounded as though she was forcing herself to remain calm but I could hear the anger in her voice. She told me she had believed that Bill, as she called him, was an MOD intelligence officer and the number she had rung me on was an MOD emergency line that she had been told by him never to use. She had decided that something was not right and called anyway; she had broken the rules of her 'training', something I had never done. There was a note of desperation in her voice – as if she needed to learn as much as possible before discovery.

I was in shock, so when Michelle asked if she could visit me, I automatically said yes and gave her my address. I wonder now if I did not think at all – but, in fact, I could not think. I had been transported away from my reality; the world I had lived in did not exist and I was left in limbo, unaware of anything other than that all had gone. Without thinking about the possible implications or consequences, I just accepted and meekly allowed the world to disintegrate around me. Michelle gave me specific instructions to tell no one – 'No one,' she emphasised – and hung up to drive up to Edinburgh.

Once again, someone was telling me to stay silent, but this time I would not do as I was told. I called a friend, a good friend who had stood by me, and I asked for help for the first time. She instantly dropped what she was doing and came to me, and I told her everything. I told her the whole story from the very beginning . . .

PART ONE:
SPOOKED

1

The First Email

November 2000

In November 2000, I was a thirty-five-year-old single mum. It had taken me over a year to get used to this title and all that it meant. I had to re-form my own perception of its significance, as I had never thought that I would find myself in this position and had remained in a miserable relationship for a year longer than I probably should have, simply because I did not want to have this label attached to me.

When my daughter Robyn was nine months old, I finally realised that by remaining where I was, feeling wretched and merely putting up with the situation, I was teaching her to behave the same way in the future. As her mother, I taught her the norms – and I was saying that it was OK to remain static even if unhappy. My attitude changed – no longer was I prepared to sacrifice myself to keep the family together; I was now determined to live as an example to my wonderful daughter. She deserved so much more than what I had found and I desperately wanted to ensure that she would grow up to have more respect for herself. I realised that if I did not show her the way, she would be unlikely to find it. If I wanted a better life for her, I had to find a better life for myself.

So I made the decision to end the relationship, and time moved on. I had a good job and was surviving financially despite my change in circumstances. I had tried the online dating thing and met three men. The first chap was lovely and became a good friend, but I wasn't physically attracted to him; the second was a man who hated his ex so vehemently that he came across like an obsessive axe murderer and I escaped our one date glad to still be alive; and the third guy I dated for several months before it became clear that he was a social parasite just looking for a new life and an easy introduction into a new world. So I gave up on online dating and became happy and settled with being single. Actually, in some ways I had never been happier, and I stayed that way for some time.

It was while I was in this frame of mind that fate intervened. Unbeknown to me, even if you cancel your membership to an online dating service they leave your advert online to pad out the membership, so my profile was still there:

Who am I? It is a strange question to answer. I am a creative, intelligent and fun woman, who has a passion for living life and enjoys talking to people, sharing ideas and having fun. I believe in positive thinking and personal responsibility, i.e. looking to the future and taking command of my own destiny rather than looking back and blaming others for things that go wrong. I like people and finding out what makes them happy, and I wake up every day believing that something wonderful is going to happen.

I love dancing Ceroc (a cross between jive and Latin American dancing), which is very sociable, fun and good exercise. I also love skiing, rock-climbing (though I am

not very good), horse-riding, swimming, music, films,
theatre, nights in, etc. – pretty much most things.

What am I looking for? Well . . . I am not altogether sure.
I have a baby daughter who will soon be one. I would
like to have a stable relationship with a caring, intelli-
gent, playful guy who would be able to take me out and
have fun, but who would also understand that I have a
baby whom I totally adore. Ideally I would like to know
someone well before getting into a relationship and am
therefore more interested in friendship at the moment.
My ideal man would be taller than me (i.e. over 5'10");
enjoy dancing (or is prepared to learn); would enjoy talk-
ing about the meaning of life; be open to other people's
opinions; have fun; and be able to play. Looks aren't all
that important, though a love of life and living are.

Regardless of whether you contact me (with photo if pos-
sible), I hope that something wonderful happens to you
today.

Out of the blue on 16 November 2000, I received a long, chatty
email from a chap called Will Allen.

The tone of his message was very relaxed and friendly. He com-
plimented me on my ad and commented that it was very different
to the others that he had read online. He told me apologetically
that he was an American but lived in the UK now and spent most
of his time in Edinburgh. He explained that he owned his own IT
consulting firm and said that he had spent most of his life up to
this point 'chasing my career around the globe'.

Will didn't have a profile on the online dating site and told
me a work colleague had emailed him about the site. He had been

killing time waiting for a business call and hadn't expected to see anyone who felt so right, so felt compelled to contact me.

He told me that he agreed with my views on personal responsibility, which is why he tried not to complain about not having a 'special someone', but recently the idea of sharing his life had become more and more important to him. Perhaps, he suggested, at thirty-four his own biological clock was ticking louder than he would care to admit.

He went on to describe himself, saying that he was 6'1", so definitely taller than me. He was mixed race, with curly hair, brown eyes and an athletic build. He said that he was reasonably well educated and was interested in art, music and literature; he even loved to dance, but although he had tried to learn Latin dance during two years in Buenos Aires, he had failed miserably!

Will stated that he wanted to make it clear from the outset that he was seeking a long-term relationship – a quick 'fun-seeker' would not find him desirable. 'My years showing me up', he supposed. That said, he also wanted to make it clear that a physical relationship was important to him as he was a very tactile person, and he realised that this might put some people off.

He then went on to say: 'It would be unfair of me to not tell you at the outset that I cannot have children of my own due to a rather unfortunate bout of mumps as a very young child, so if growing your family naturally is on your cards, then I suppose that I am not the best choice of partners.' While he was very keen to have children, and got on very well with them, he said he'd had to 'adjust to the fact that I will not have my own biological family and that has been harder at some times than at others. It's not baggage at all, just reality.'

He wrote some more and then signed off, saying that he would love to meet up sometime for a coffee and a chat but if I was not interested, then he would at least wish me the very best of luck in my future.

We emailed daily, twice daily, three times – back and forth, flirting, chatting and telling each other more and more about ourselves. All of it wonderful, exciting and new. I stayed calm, as I had been here before and was determined not to get too wrapped up in the anticipation in case I was disappointed when we met. But it was all so natural, easy even, and just felt right. Nearly two weeks passed and we knew so much about each other, had shared many intimate details and still we liked each other.

Then came the line that was inevitable: maybe we should talk on the phone.

Absolutely. I gave him my number and he promised to call within half an hour.

I waited. No call came.

I emailed asking if he was OK. No answer. I emailed again. I was starting to worry. What on earth could have happened? There was no indication of any hesitancy or doubt in his suggestion to call – he had asked for my number, he had enthusiastically requested it and stated wholeheartedly that he wanted to ring, yet no call came. It made no sense at all.

I fretted all night and went to work the next day anxious. I thought about it constantly, going over and over his emails and trying to understand what could have happened, then reading my own again to see if I'd said anything that could have been misconstrued. Nothing.

I emailed again, asking if he was OK. I had images in my head of him having fallen downstairs and broken his neck. What could have made him vanish within half an hour of sending that message?

Two days later, he got in touch again.

'Sorry, had to go on a business trip to Spain.'

I was really annoyed. I told him I had been worried and under no circumstances was it OK. I told him to get lost.

He apologised and said he had misunderstood the timescale. He had been distracted by a business call, then had to hurriedly pack and depart. He said he'd thought of me the whole time and missed me. He gave me his number and begged me to phone, saying it was just bad timing and circumstances; he repeatedly emphasised that he really did want to talk to me.

Initially I ignored him and refused to talk, but he kept apologising and promising that it had not been intentional. Eventually I decided that if he was that keen, maybe I should give him a second chance. I calmed down and we arranged that he would ring me that night. At that stage, I was so angry that I did not care if he called or not. But he did and we talked just as naturally as we had via email. I grudgingly forgave him for causing me to worry, but I teased him and said he'd better not do it again. He swore he never would and promised to be more considerate in future.

We talked for hours during that first call. He was very open about being infertile and how it had affected his life. Family meant everything to Will. His sister was very important to him and he talked with pride about his mother's intelligence and how loyal and loving his dad was. He told me how it saddened him that he wasn't able to have a son to carry on the family name. He would have loved to have had a family of his own but when he found out he was unable to have kids he had turned his focus to his career, becoming a bit of a workaholic. He'd only had one long-term relationship and that had ended because she'd wanted kids. It was his baggage but he had come to terms with it.

The conversation flowed easily and he seemed really interested and attentive. I liked his voice: it was calm, smooth and articulate. His American accent was gentle rather than brash and the edges had been worn down by the eight years he had spent in the UK. He had residency here because of his work and intended to stay because he liked it and it was a good base. He travelled all the time throughout the UK, but mostly between Manchester and Edinburgh, as he had an office and staff based in St Andrew Square in Edinburgh but his main client was a company in Manchester.

Will admitted that work had been his life, day and night. With the advent of the 24/7 business culture, communication and IT had to be running all the time, and people were used to him being on call and constantly available to sort out problems. He ran an IT consultancy and communications firm, and one service he offered to clients was to hack into their IT systems to see how secure they were. It was interesting stuff.

I tried to find out more about Will on the Internet and did searches with the information I had. Unfortunately, 'Will Allen' brought up a plethora of references and even adding 'IT consultant' to the search did not help, as it was still too general.

Will sent me a photograph of himself and I sent him one of me. He was extremely flattering about mine and I was nervous about looking at his. Eventually, however, I opened the file to see a nice face looking back at me. He was not stunning but certainly good-looking, with a warm smile, mixed-race colouring, dark eyes and short-cropped Afro hair. The glasses – wire-framed US Air Force-type with slightly rose-tinted lenses – struck me as very 1980s. The photo didn't reveal God's gift to women but he did look gentle and attractive. I showed the photograph to a couple of my friends who laughed at the glasses but otherwise said he looked quite nice.

By the first week of December 2000, we were talking on the phone and emailing several times a day, and very quickly I was feeling very connected to him. He agreed with my philosophy and we discussed our common beliefs at length, including books we'd both read and loved. Our phone calls were always long and we were never lost for things to talk about.

2

THE FIRST MEETING

December 2000

Now that we were communicating regularly, it seemed only natural that we would meet up, so we arranged a lunch date in early December 2000. Always slightly cautious, I wanted to meet in a public place, during daylight hours and with other people around. I was nobody's fool and did not want to put myself at risk – I had met the suspected mad axe murderer, after all, and I did not want to go through that again! Will, therefore, had my mobile number and I his, but as yet he did not have my address or any further details.

I spent some time getting ready for our first date, thinking about the immense possibility the meeting could hold and also the immense potential for disappointment if this man did not turn out to be the person he seemed online. I felt such a closeness to him, a real connection, and I almost did not want to spoil that by meeting him. How could he live up to the idea I had of him? I was happy and settled: I was secure and comfortable with my life as it was. Falling for another man would only put that security at risk, but the possibility of finding happiness and meeting someone who would make me feel like a woman again was irresistible. So I got ready, and then changed, then got changed again – eventually and predictably ending up in the outfit that I had put on first.

I arrived on schedule at his plush office in St Andrew Square; the reception was on the second floor, so I took the lift. The doors opened on to a big, modern, open reception area with high ceilings and curved leather armchairs. There were two or three enormous widescreen TVs set on *CNN* and a lone, smartly dressed girl behind a large reception desk. It was quite an impressive scene.

I approached the desk.

'Hi,' I said as confidently as I could. 'I'm here to meet Will Allen.'

She looked blank, searched her screen and said, 'We don't have a Will Allen working here.'

I had no doubt that I had the right place, so I gave her a description of him. 'Well, I'm sure I have the right place. Can you just check for me, please? He's a tall, mixed-race American chap.'

'Oh, that would be Will Jordan,' she said. 'I'll let him know you're here.'

I sat down and waited, pondering the different name. How had that happened? His email definitely said that he was Will Allen, but then maybe he was nervous about giving out his real name online. If so, that would explain why I had not managed to find any information about him on the Web.

The doors opened and closed a few times, my heart jumping on each occasion, but it was not him. Then the lift doors opened again and he walked out.

He strode towards me, flashing a set of white teeth, his smile broad and warm. I was instantly drawn to his quietly confident, relaxed manner, his tall, dark-skinned, muscular body and his attractive features. The glasses he wore were very old-fashioned but did not detract from his overall good looks. There he was, finally coming towards me in physical form. I returned his smile and he

15

took my hand with a firm but unpressurised grip as I stood, then he kissed me very gently on the cheek as we said hello.

'Shall we go?' he said, and we moved back to the lift. We were going to a restaurant nearby for lunch.

'How come your name is Jordan, not Allen?' I asked almost immediately.

'Oh, Allen is my middle name,' he said, without a glance or pause.

We had a pleasant two-hour lunch and at one point discussed books we'd read, notably *The Celestine Prophecy*. In this book, the author talks about people connecting through sharing their physical and emotional energy; he says that you can feel this energy flowing between you when you are near each other, and this creates a bond. I asked how, within that philosophy, it was possible to feel this energy over email. This was something that we both agreed had happened, but it defied the rationale. Will looked like he'd been struck by lightning. During all our time together, he would refer to that as being the moment he fell in love with me – the moment when he realised he'd found his soulmate.

As he'd told me, Will was about six feet tall and athletic. He described his background and how he had two white grandfathers, one Native American grandmother and one Afro-Caribbean grandmother. Both his grandfathers had been ahead of their time by marrying women of different colour, despite the prevailing social norms. He joked, 'The only thing I inherited from the Native American side was their lack of tolerance for alcohol.'

Will also had very little facial hair but told me he had recently been trying to cultivate a moustache, of which he was very proud. It was more of a bum-fluff type of thing but he said he had never had to shave due to low testosterone levels caused by the mumps he'd had as a child. (I found out later, when our relationship became sexual, that he had no hair on his chest either.) He was excited

16

about the idea of being able to grow a beard, but at the moment there was no hair growing on his chin. I found his enthusiasm for the subject endearing and even felt a bit sorry for him.

The conversation was animated and alive. He was interested in what I had to say and we had so much in common – what we believed in, what we had read. Here was a successful, attractive, ordinary, interesting guy who seemed to be interested in me. But still I held back. I told him I had a wonderful life and that if he wanted to be part of it he would have to improve it, which would be a tall order. He said that he understood, and laughed, saying he would have to think about how to do that!

He walked me back to my car, my arm tucked in his, and as we stopped to part ways he leaned forward and kissed me gently on the lips. I noticed how soft his lips were, and it was clear that had I leaned into him the kiss would have deepened and continued. I held back, though, and we parted, said goodbye and I drove away.

He emailed me only a couple of hours after I'd left, saying that his heart had only finally stopped racing and that, to be honest, he was finding it hard to keep his feet on the ground. He seemed to be taken aback by the intensity of his feelings and was nervous that I might not feel the same way. He went back to the comment I had made at lunch about the way we had felt a connection to one another even via email, and reiterated that he had known from our first messages that he was going to like me.

He went on to say that nothing could have prepared him for the moment he stepped out of the elevator, when he thought to himself, *'Even prettier than her picture'*, then signed off by saying that he imagined his lips were still tingling after our parting kiss and that he could not wait to see me again. 'Until we speak again, have a great weekend and know that you are in my thoughts and dreams.'

Things moved fast from then on. Will emailed daily and got more and more enthusiastic about our relationship. I felt relaxed with this man, and although I'd only met him once I felt a real connection with him. He was clearly not a threatening type but was quiet, intelligent and solid.

A few days later, for our second date, I invited him over for lunch. He came to my lovely old first-floor tenement flat overlooking the sea in Portobello. I am a dreadful cook and the pasta I cooked him was barely edible, made much worse by a business call he received in the middle of eating it. He was on the phone for forty minutes and walked through to the other room to talk. He made an apologetic face and I tried not to be irritated – after all, it was business. We talked again for a couple of hours and I showed him some family photos, including ones of my daughter. Eventually it was time to pick up Robyn, then one year old, from her nursery and before we left the flat he kissed me.

He wrapped his arms around my waist and pulled me to him. He confidently pressed his lips on to mine and I felt the softness again, but this time he was more determined. I sank into his arms and actually felt my knees buckle as his kiss overtook me. It left me dishevelled and breathless, and awoke emotions that had been buried for a long time.

Will and I saw each other every couple of days, and with each meeting we felt more and more intensely about each other. I received a dozen gorgeous red roses at work, which caused great interest among my colleagues – particularly as I had not mentioned having a new man in my life. Will would send me cards with romantic sentiments as well as finding other ways to tell me constantly how he was falling in love with me.

Will was so considerate and demonstrated his affection in a million tiny ways. I remember once sitting in the car with him, sharing a bottle of water and, even though he was clearly thirsty, he made sure that he left the last bit for me. He would automatically open the car door for me and walk on the outside of the pavement – things that my mother had told me mattered, which showed him to be a well-mannered person. I was touched by this sort of gentle thoughtfulness and by the way he took care to show me every day that he was thinking of me. He would text to say he missed me, call to say what his work colleagues were saying about his 'mysterious girlfriend', and email jokes and things he wanted to share that he'd come across.

Will was unlike anyone I had ever dated before. He was intelligent and accomplished but humble about his achievements. For instance, when in my living room he noticed my piano and mentioned quietly that he could play. I had a degree in music and was classically trained on the piano; I had played Beethoven in concerts from the age of about eleven. When I asked him to play for me, however, I found that he was considerably better than I. He played a whole range of different styles flawlessly but was constantly self-critical, saying that he was technically good but musically poor. The truth was, he was brilliant. He also played the guitar well, along with various other instruments.

He was talented in other areas as well, speaking nine languages fluently, including Hebrew, and could speed read a book in the most amazingly short time. His knowledge of computers and communications seemed extraordinary. He was very confident in that field, talking about advances in technology and the types of things that IT could achieve. He was very technically minded, sorting out my computer system to work more efficiently and even designing and uploading a website for Robyn and me.

Whereas I was boisterous and a performer, quick to laugh and see the funny side, Will was quiet, almost shy, but with a solid confidence, totally devoid of arrogance, in everything he did. He had done so much, travelling and working all over the world. He was a man you could look up to: attractive, fit and strong, mentally quick without being a show-off, creative and sensual, romantic and thoughtful without being soppy. He seemed to be an anomaly, a different breed of man altogether.

Will's only fault at this stage seemed to be timekeeping, as he continually turned up late and occasionally did not show at all. Sometimes he would disappear for days at a time and I would worry about him. When this happened, it was hard to accept, but Will told me that he was also finding it hard and tried to keep me informed about his movements. It caused us to row, but he would apologise and explain how hard he was trying.

On one occasion, not long after we met, my brother invited Will and I to dinner. He wanted to meet my new chap and we arranged to go. At the last minute, Will got caught up in work and had to pull out. I was deeply embarrassed but had to put a brave face on it. Will, as always, was extremely apologetic and made it up to me again later the same night. He said he was working to improve the situation and told me that things would change when people realised he actually had a life outside work now.

The same thing happened a couple of times when Will had been due to go to a social event with me or we had arranged to meet up with my friends. I started to get teased about my absent man, the joke being that I had an imaginary boyfriend. Inwardly, I found it incredibly frustrating: I had found the perfect man but I couldn't show him off. Each and every time it happened he promised he would never do it again.

The friends who had met him were impressed. They liked him and commented on how obvious his affection for me was. When I was with Will, he had eyes for only me. Unlike some men, he would not look at other women or even seem to notice them. He made me feel so special.

I was very aware of the effect that bringing a new man into our lives might have on my baby and for that reason hadn't taken home any of the other men I had dated. But it was swiftly becoming clear that this was a serious relationship, albeit early days, so I introduced my daughter to Will and they seemed to get on very well. Will adored Robyn and she took to him as well. Because he was infertile, it meant a lot to him that I already had a child. He talked about her and how much he adored her and me. He was attentive and enthusiastic and interested in my child – just a wonderful boyfriend.

I only wished that we could spend more time together. Then, just before Christmas, it seemed that things were about to get better. Will had been invited to a big event in London: it was a black-tie do with his biggest client and would mean dressing up and staying over at a five-star hotel. Will asked me to go with him and I was thrilled. It wasn't often, if ever, that I got the opportunity to travel, to dress up, to be pampered and to feel like a woman again for a couple of days rather than only a mum. I jumped at the chance and set about organising time off work, and asked my mum to take Robyn overnight so I could go.

On the day itself, 23 December 2000, my bags were packed and waiting by the door long before they needed to be. We were getting a 4 p.m. flight and I emailed Will throughout the day to share my excitement and remind him not to be late or we'd miss the plane. He was supposed to be finishing work at lunchtime so we would have plenty of time, but I was nervous that he would let work take precedence again. I waited and then texted as time drew on.

Yes, yes . . . patience, I got back. *Just finishing now, be there in half an hour.* He was cutting it fine . . . He was cutting it finer still . . . He did not arrive but was still on his way . . . He was sorting out another flight . . . Then he just went quiet.

I was heartbroken. He didn't show and now his phone was switched off. I eventually had a drink – actually I drank a whole bottle of wine – and went to bed feeling disappointed and confused. It was too late to pick up my daughter, so I would do that in the morning.

The next day was Christmas Eve, and before I went to get Robyn I got a sheepish call from Will asking if he could come over. He told me he had something to say, and I wanted to know what had mattered more than me and all the effort I had put into the trip. I was so angry I could hardly speak, and I wanted an explanation.

He arrived and apologised. Something had come up at work: a client had panicked and pulled the plug on a whole business system, and he'd spent the whole night working in their basement trying to sort it out. There was no mobile phone signal and he'd got so involved he'd not thought of another way to get in touch. I was not happy.

Then he told me that he was upset about missing the trip, too, because he'd planned to do something while we were away. Still annoyed, I asked what. In response, he gave me a teddy bear with a diamond ring attached to a ribbon around its neck. He asked me to marry him.

I was blindsided. I stood in my kitchen leaning against the cooker, ankles and arms crossed. I had to untangle my arms to take the teddy bear, and in the process my annoyance and frustration dissipated as the conversation took a new direction. I was hesitant, but he went on to tell me his reasons for wanting to marry me, and kept us on this new path.

We had been together such a short time and here was a man I adored who had fallen head over heels in love with me. It was intoxicating, exciting and immensely enticing. I knew I was in love with him, too, but I also knew that we had not had enough time to get to know one another. I said I would think about it and he said, 'OK, as long as you wear the ring while you think about it.' So I did, and from then on the question was never raised except as a fait accompli. The wedding was on.

◆　◆　◆

Will had to work over Christmas. He'd planned to join our big family gathering, but again work intervened and he did not arrive. I had a miserable time being teased about his absence and having to defend his obsession with work, when in truth I was just as pissed off as everyone else. But Will was very reserved and I figured that he was holding back from meeting them partly because of nerves.

I did, however, wear the ring that Will had given me, as requested. I told my family that he had proposed, but I was thinking about it. They were pleased for me, but more pleased that I was being sensible about holding off. Meanwhile, the introductions would just have to wait; I knew they'd happen eventually.

In January 2001, I discovered my daughter was going to have a baby half-sibling by her father's new girlfriend, Linda.

I emailed Will about it.

Robyn is going to have a little brother or sister.

And before you jump to any odd conclusions! Ross's girl-friend, Linda, is pregnant. It will be interesting to see what happens. I have promised Linda that I will help out as much as possible, poor thing is going to have it tough, I think. I am glad that Robyn is going to have a sibling, though.

Will's reply was both articulate and emotional. The message had obviously given him a big shock and he said that he had spent about a minute in a state of bliss, thinking that by some act of God I was pregnant.

He'd had an extreme physical reaction to the news, feeling each heartbeat pounding in his chest; the blood rushing to his head had sounded like a train. The guys he was with thought he was having a heart attack and made him sit down, but when his vision had cleared and everyone had stopped panicking, he read on and realised the true situation.

It was clear that Will wished he had been the one to give Robyn her next brother or sister. He told me how he would have considered it a 'tremendous blessing' to make love and then wait for the end of the month to buy pregnancy tests. He would have given anything to share that moment of knowing that he had been part of creating a new life and had imagined how he would feel if I was carrying our baby.

The message had clearly hit a nerve, leading him to say: 'I'm sorry, I promised myself that I would not get upset about this, but it is so hard not to be bitter . . .' His email was long and passionate, saying that I was now woven into the very fabric of his being. He said: 'I truly hope that, if you don't already, you never come to resent me or to think of me as less of a man because I cannot do this. I know that my heart could never take that, coming from you . . . please don't measure me by that one failing that I can do nothing about.'

Still in the same email, Will went on to talk about the intensity of his feelings the first time we made love. He said it had shown him the two furthest extremes of emotion he had ever experienced: how much he had come to love me and wanted to be bound to me for life, and the abject frustration and despair of knowing that he had finally found all that he had ever wanted in a wife and mother of his children, but that the second part of that dream could never happen. He felt as if he had spent his whole life preparing to make the commitment that would mark the end of 'his' life and the beginning of the life that he would share completely with another person. But whatever plans or dreams he had, they would not change the fact that he could not father children.

He ended the email by saying that my love for him had helped him to deal with his pain, and he repeated once more how much he loved me with words that melted my heart. He said that there were just no words that could express how strongly he felt, or enough room in one email to hold them if there were: 'It genuinely frightens me to try to comprehend the depth of my feelings for you because I never knew it was possible to feel this way about anyone.'

The strength of emotion in Will's emails touched me greatly. I wanted so much to give him a child, to heal all that hurt which ran so deep, but I knew I couldn't change nature.

What also came through loud and clear at this time were Will's feelings about infidelity and the male mind. We had talked at length about our previous relationships, mostly mine as he'd had very few due to work commitments, and he told me repeatedly that he could not understand how a man could have children with a woman and walk away; he felt it was 'evil and mocking in the greatest of ways, made even worse by the complete lack of reverence it shows'. If there was one thing I felt certain of, therefore, it was that unfaithfulness went against everything that Will held dear – it would be anathema to him. Here was a man I could be sure of, a man who was monogamous, loyal and had values.

3

SPOOKED

January 2001

Although I was convinced by Will's displays of emotion and reassured by his convictions about fidelity, I continued to be less than impressed by his punctuality and reliability when it came to meeting up. Again and again, plans were made and then he'd be late or simply not show. He was still loving and devoted to me, and adored Robyn, but he seemed to be so focused on his work all the time that he just didn't think to remember his personal commitments. I suspected the situation was made worse by the fact that he didn't have a fixed abode. He told me that he rented a storeroom for his stuff and stayed in hotels, so we set about finding him a flat that would reduce his storage costs and give him a base.

In the back of my mind, though, I had the feeling that something wasn't right. Will had changed his mobile phone a couple of times since I had met him, saying that his company was changing providers and that I should use the new number. Gradually, I grew suspicious. There was something very odd about all this, and by the end of January I was determined to get to the bottom of it.

He had created a personal website for me, so I looked it up on www.WHOis.net and found details of his business and an address in Lancashire. I pulled the Company House records for his business and found he was the company secretary; a woman called Michelle Hayward was listed as a director. Her address was in Lancashire but his was listed in a village outside Edinburgh. I agonised over what to do but I had to know, so I got in the car and drove there.

I found the address easily in a quiet, leafy backstreet of Gullane, close to the sea and in an area of high-walled private suburban houses. I drove past three times before stopping the car and, while sitting outside, it crossed my mind that the residents in the area would think I was casing the street. I was actually nervous that someone might phone the police.

Eventually I got out and walked up to the gate in the high wall. I could see through to a large, quite grand, detached house surrounded by garden. Will was away in Manchester but there in the drive was parked his two-seater black Corvette. The greatest shock, however, was the children's play equipment in the garden – the preschool climbing frame and toys.

A flurry of thoughts swirled through my mind as I tried to make sense of what I was seeing. The one thing I had previously felt absolutely sure of was that Will would not be unfaithful to me. His views on the subject were very pronounced and he just did not seem the type at all. But this was too much. I had to know for sure what was going on.

I wandered around and found a passing local. I said I was working on locating property for a client and this was the ideal house; did they know who owned it?

'No,' he said. 'Probably some family, but everyone pretty much keeps themselves to themselves in the area.'

I went home. I couldn't see any activity within the house and I had no desire at all to knock on the door.

I called Will on his mobile the minute I walked through the door, and he answered.

'We need to talk, now!' I said.

'What's happened?'

'Just come and talk to me.' I wanted to see him face to face, see his eyes and know the truth.

He set off almost immediately and was with me within hours.

'It's not what you think,' he said. 'Oh, God.' I had challenged him with what I had seen and done. 'Right, hold on.'

He took his phone and went through to the other room, leaving me on hold, confused, upset and hurting but with a modicum of hope. Could there be some other explanation for what I had seen?

He was on the phone for what seemed like an age. I could hear him talking but it wasn't possible to make out what he was saying. Then he came back and sat me down to tell me the truth. He started with, 'Before you say anything, just hear me out.'

Will then went on to tell me that he was an intelligence officer for the US government, based and working in Europe. His specialist area was Europe but at present he was focusing on the Israel/Palestine issue, which was what the majority of his team were working on. He was not a 'front guy' but had more of a support role; he'd not managed to go further up the ladder because of his inability to drink alcohol without getting uncontrollably chatty – something I already knew about him. He'd worked for a couple of years in Japan and again in Brazil, as well as various other places around the world, and his particular area of expertise was PCs and IT.

He talked for hours, telling me details of his training and the work he had done, including the setting up of websites the FBI had used to shut down paedophile rings. Anyone who accessed the target site picked up hidden software and was tracked back to their own system. After that, the authorities could track their emails and other sites accessed, meaning that everyone involved in the ring could be identified and caught. They'd shut down a particularly famous ring that way, and this was especially pertinent to me as I had been a victim of child molestation at the hands of a family friend, though Will did not know this at the time. Here was someone actively doing something to counteract the abuse these people were dealing out.

He told me how the company he currently headed in Edinburgh was an ordinary IT consultancy but was also used as a front to provide Will with contracts as a security consultant. This work gave him access to assess the IT security of specific systems, because how better to bug and infiltrate a company and find out if they were involved in supporting terrorism than to hack into their system; and how better to hack into their system than by being paid by the company to do so?

When he was called away, he was not allowed to tell me; he just had to go, no matter what was happening in his personal life. Our security depended on it. This was not a game or a joke, but real and solid. As he explained the situation, we were both sitting on the couch; he was holding my hands and looking clearly and steadily into my eyes. While he was talking to me, my phone started to beep with incoming text messages. Again and again it said 'SIM Update', and Will told me that these software updates altered the phone's status, saying, 'It will make the phone traceable and keep you safe by allowing the agency to tap into the phone itself.'

Before I could question how it would keep me safe he moved on to another point, overwhelming me with more and more information.

He showed me the ODCI website, ODCI standing for the Official Department of Central Intelligence – the inside name for the CIA. Then he showed me around the site to places not accessible to the public, while I received another series of texts from 'ODCI RELAY'. There was no number, no information and no return path, just automated programme chip updates that changed the settings and information contained within the phone's software.

The house in Gullane was the Scottish base for the team, ideally located near the sea and in a quiet area where people kept themselves to themselves. Did I notice all the antennae on the roof? he asked.

'Yes, I did,' I admitted.

'More than just for a family, huh?' he asked.

'Yes,' I said. 'But what about the children's play equipment?'

'For show, so that people make the same assumption you did: that a family live there. Listen, Mary, now you are on the inside you won't have to take anything on faith; it won't just be my word, you'll get firm proof and meet some of the other people involved. You will need to be security checked properly, but then all will become much clearer.'

I then asked him who Michelle Hayward was and he told me that she was a friend who had helped him set up in business. She was someone he had previously worked with and fronted the business in name only, because in his line of work it was best not to have a trail leading back to your real home.

There was no hint of nervousness or discomfort as he spoke. His eyes were soft, warm and, as always, loving and kind.

I was not a 100 per cent hooked, but I did believe him. Here was this mild-mannered, deep, emotional, humble and loving man, who seemed intelligent, loyal and devoted to what he believed in, telling me the most fantastic story I had ever heard, opening up a whole new world. It was a world that I knew existed but I had not expected to be exposed to it in any way.

On the one hand, I couldn't help but think that he fitted the description and personality of someone who'd do this kind of work, and he was telling me about it all without a hint of bragging or humour. He was deadly serious and matter-of-fact, while staring unflinchingly into my eyes. He was mildly irritated with himself for having let things get to this stage and was so used to keeping it all under wraps that he found it difficult to talk about. But he persevered through the awkwardness, answering the questions that he could.

On the other hand, it could all be a lie and he could be married with kids. But that would mean he had been lying from the very first email – that everything I knew about him, down to the smallest and deepest detail, was false and twisted. He was not the type. Will's emails were always eloquent, expressive and emotional. Indeed, the depth of his emotions had bowled me over. My previous relationship had been with someone who did not express himself, or indeed make me feel loved at all. Will made me feel loved and valued; when he was with me he made me feel like I was the only aspect of his life that mattered. I had already started to crave that attention and felt totally alone and isolated when he was away.

The whole situation stunned me and I did not know what to think. I ran it all through my mind repeatedly. Someone did this job and I could think of no one more suited to it than him. He had assured me that I would not have to take his word for it but would see the proof for myself soon enough – I would meet others and know for sure. So, although I might not have been totally convinced, I was more inclined to believe than not. I knew this man. What would he have lied to me for? What on earth would he have achieved long term?

That night he cried as he held me. He was upset that he'd come so close to losing me and we swore to love each other, always and forever, no matter what.

Now I understood why he'd vanish, things changed a bit. I stopped giving him so much grief about it. After all, he was off saving the world, keeping us all safe. It was like living with Superman: how could you complain about him not turning up to dinner when he was holding up a collapsing bridge and saving lives? He relaxed a lot with me as well, because he didn't have to hide so much. He became less guarded and started to include me in some ways, not telling me about his work but how he felt about it.

I spoke to a couple of his colleagues – a man and a woman that he worked with. We didn't discuss any details about his work but they would call to tell me that he was away and pass on messages to me. I suggested a couple of times to Will that we meet up with them but he told me that neither of them were people he would socialise with.

Will carried a gun for quite a while and needed to lock this up when off duty. I never actually saw it and he didn't mention it to me. I asked about it because, after the revelations, I had felt it through his jacket more than once when I hugged him and I had seen the holster when I walked in on him changing one day. I did ask to see it because I was curious (although the very idea terrified me) but he refused to show me, saying that it was absolutely forbidden by the CIA to brandish it about. Whenever he was carrying it while visiting me, he would ask for the key to the hall cupboard and it would immediately be locked away from 'civilian harm', as he put it – something that made me more comfortable because, although I had no doubts about his ability to protect us and keep us safe, I was seriously unhappy about having a gun on the premises at all, especially near a small child.

Will told me he did not get paid directly by the CIA because payslips and bank accounts are too easy to trace. Instead, he and other operatives were given anything they wanted to carry out their work – clothes, cars, gadgets and even houses.

When we met, he was driving the black Corvette I had seen parked outside the house in Gullane, but shortly afterwards this disappeared and was replaced by what he called his latest 'work vehicle'. It was like a tank that you had to climb up into – a black 4x4 with tinted windows. That car lasted for about a year before just disappearing back from whence it came.

He had an apartment in Spain, which was his retreat, and he promised us a visit there very soon. He also had a house in the US that his aunt had left him. His mother suffered from severe depression and was often in hospital, so his father concentrated on looking after her, and Will's aunt had often been a surrogate mother to him and his sister. For some reason I could never quite grasp if his sister was older or younger than him.

Will was also issued with a cash card – a hole-in-the-wall card with which he could take out £300 per day 'expenses'. So he was never short of money. He promised that 'if nothing else' we would be able to live on his 'expenses card' alone. However, this depended on him being around to access the hole in the wall.

Will had warned me that I would be rigorously security checked and told me it was likely that I would be watched and even followed. He had already told me that the SIM updates had made my phone traceable in case I was kidnapped by any 'unsavouries', and this was technology I had heard about. But now he warned me that nothing said around the mobile was ever private; sound could be picked up from the phone as long as it had battery power, even if it wasn't switched on.

More than anything it was the details that proved he was what he said he was that finally made me believe him wholeheartedly. The constant mobile-phone SIM updates; the texts from anonymous sources only entitled 'ODCI RELAY' or 'MOD RELAY'; the emails he sent me from the field, which when I checked the path came through www.field-odci.net, which looked authentic to me, and www.odci.gov (which was the CIA website at the time); the cash he produced sealed in plastic wallets printed with the Ministry of Defence logo; the gun that I had often felt through his jacket and the holster that I saw; the pass and parking permit for RAF Brize Norton; the gadgets and mobile phones; the people who would call to tell me he was unavailable or called away; the secret calls; the language he used; and the watch! His watch was amazing, and was pure black with the Rado logo on it. It would vibrate to wake him up and, half asleep, he would say he'd been paged and had to leave. He would then fall back into bed and back to sleep, and sometime later a more aggressive buzz would make him jump up. I asked how they knew he was not up and he sleepily explained that the watch had GPS – global positioning system – inside, which meant they knew he wasn't moving. He was rarely allowed to take his watch off, and if he didn't it meant he might leave at any second. I hated that watch with a justifiable passion, as it took him away from me.

He was physically very fit and super-confident about his abilities. He demonstrated martial arts moves to me and was able to kick-jump a target over six feet in the air. We play-fought defensive moves and he showed me holds and how to defend myself – he was indeed very good at it. I'd had some training when I worked as a security guard (i.e. a bouncer) to pay the bills while I was at college, so I knew some of the stuff already. He told me how he had been screen-tested for a martial arts film when he was eighteen, and that his mother still had the video. He would get her to send it over so I could see it. I received a few emails from his mother, who said that she was very happy to know that Will was settled and had a stepdaughter he could call his own; she even promised that she would send over some old photographs of him.

Another detail was his driving. He would rarely signal or wear a seatbelt and used to leave the engine running when filling up with petrol. Everything was about speed, not being followed and manoeuvrability. I felt very secure when he was driving and he modestly told me of the intensive training he'd undergone. It showed: I have never known anyone more at one with a vehicle or to have more control at the wheel than he did.

I was told that I should be aware of anything odd: any odd package or any person wanting information or trying to get close to me. They were likely to make an approach by finding something in common, like a child at the same school. So I had to be suspicious of anyone new, any 'friend' who showed too much interest, any person delivering to the house or calling for 'market research' purposes. In fact, he told me, they were most likely to approach one of my sisters or a friend, someone close to me, and put a child at the nursery they used, befriending them so that further details about me could be uncovered through seemingly innocuous gossip. It was so simple – they would just mention over a cup of tea how their husband was away a lot and this would prompt my sister to talk about how her sister's fiancé was away a lot, too. I actually heard her do this a couple of times and was wary of the people she was talking to. They would turn to ask me more about it and I would shrug and say he was busy with work before swiftly changing the subject, irrationally irritated with my sister. It was not her fault, he assured me; it is a normal human reaction and something we all tend to do – we share what we have in common, discuss similarities. That is why the intelligence services use that technique.

The only way to stay safe was to keep everything to myself, to keep silent. I had to ensure that Robyn stayed safe, too. I could talk to Will, as he was my friend and my confidant; he was the only one that I could be open with and whom I could trust.

My friends and family did not understand our relationship, and I could not explain. They were getting suspicious about his failure to show up for family events and my friends continued to tease me about my imaginary boyfriend. In February 2001, however,

Will finally met the majority of my family, though my sister Lisa was away living with her husband in Japan. It was at this point that he asked my father formally for my hand in marriage. After meeting him, my family did seem to feel a bit better about the situation. They found Will charming; even my mother liked him, which was important to me as we were very close and she had never particularly liked any of my previous boyfriends. They were pleased to see me so happy and glad that I had found someone who I wanted to settle down with, though this might not have been the case if they had known what Will really did for a living.

It was so frustrating not being able to explain the full story to people, but this was not a game and not something I could just blurt out. My increasing wariness and paranoia alienated me from many people and strengthened the bond I had with Will.

He gave me hints and techniques on how to tell if I was being followed and what to do, but if anything odd happened, I was to report to him immediately. If he was out of the country, his phone was monitored back at base and I was still to leave a voicemail message.

I was followed once and did as I had been told. I walked away without giving any sign that I had spotted the man tailing me and quickly ducked behind a wall, taking off my jacket and hat and letting my hair loose. The chap passed me, looking frantically to see where I had gone, and I stepped back into the road to follow him. I wasn't trying to find out where he was going; I just wanted to know he was not behind me. I called it in while I was doing it. The chap was looking around and clocked me within a few moments. He bolted across the road and ran away down a side street. Will told me to go to a crowded public space, which I did, and then I waited for an hour in a busy cafe, watching from the window to see if there was any sign of the guy. Then Will told me to get out of there as quickly as possible, once the coast was clear.

On another occasion, I was at a theatre in the Scottish Highlands waiting for Will to arrive. He'd been saying all day that he was on his way and asked me to leave a ticket for him on the door. I did so, but by the time I reached my seat there was a chap sitting in the one next to it, holding the ticket I had left at reception. I told him it was my husband's ticket and asked him how he'd got hold of it. He told me that his name was Jordan and that the ticket had been left for him at the door. He left and got a seat elsewhere, but I was frightened. I texted Will throughout the show and he told me that it was a warning; that was why he had not come. He said I would be safe as long as he was not with me. 'They' were telling him and me that they knew where we were. I was totally spooked and in a strange town on my own. I hardly slept that night and felt very strange and exposed.

Will told me how to spot if there were people inside a surveillance vehicle, and I had to keep an eye on every potentially suspicious car or van parked outside the house. Professional surveillance people know not to move around much, but if you watch a van for long enough you can see there are people inside – the suspension shifts.

Once, my flat was burgled. My neighbour called me at work and I headed home immediately. I called Will on the way and he told me not to touch anything. He asked if the police had been called and when I said they had, he was round like a shot. He went through the whole house with a hand-held scanner, checking for bugs and surveillance gear, but decided in the end that it had just been a straightforward burglary. Strangely enough, this helped detract from the upset of being burgled, because at least it wasn't part of something bigger.

All these things were very scary, but it was also exciting. I had absolute faith that Will would protect us and keep us safe, and he had absolute confidence in his ability to do so. I did not feel enough of a big fish to mean anything to anyone and did not really feel that any harm would come to me, so it didn't feel real at all. There were times when I was frightened, but then the morning would come and I would put it all behind me and keep moving forward.

Over the years, Will told me more and more of his history: how he'd been recruited out of school because he'd got the top SAT score for the state of New Jersey. (It was at his initial CIA full medical, when he was eighteen, that they discovered he was infertile from the mumps he'd had as a child.) He'd been put through university by the service and been given a doctorate in personal computing – but he dismissed this achievement, saying computing was much simpler in the mid-1980s. He was so modest about his abilities that he did not use the title 'Dr' at all, and was actually embarrassed by it. I only ever found out about it because an administrator who booked a hotel for us in Cambridge used his full title without asking him, and even then I had to prise the information out of him.

One time, when Will had been away for a long period and out of contact, he came back and signalled to me that we couldn't talk in our house. Something had changed and he was very agitated; more noticeably, he was not wearing his glasses. We got a babysitter and went out to dinner at an Italian restaurant, where we spent the evening talking pleasantly about Robyn and my work. Throughout the whole meal, though, we were having another conversation. Will took a napkin and wrote that he was bugged and could not talk openly; he told me that he'd had laser surgery on his eyes and had gone on a mission to the Palestinian territories, though he could not tell me specifically where. The laser surgery had been necessary because he'd needed to use telescopic sights.

I went cold thinking that he might have actually been a sniper in the operation, but I did not enquire further because I didn't want to know if he had been involved in something like that and selfishly pushed it to the back of my mind. He did tell me some details about the operation, and also told me that he was only on leave for a short period of time. As the operation was still ongoing and others were still out there, he had to be bugged so they knew he was not giving out any information. He told me this because he knew I would ask questions about where he had been and why he had been out of contact, and wanted to bypass that conversation.

Being a contact lens wearer since the age of sixteen, I had often tried to persuade Will to try contacts but he felt squeamish about the idea of touching his eyes. The thought of him undergoing laser eye surgery was distressing to me, and I looked closely to see if I could detect any marks or damage to his eyes. Certainly he did not have contact lenses in, and I knew that his eyesight was so bad that he could not have driven without his glasses. Will said that the process would have to be reversed once the operation was over, but the general outcome was that he got over his fear of contact lenses and later on started to wear monthly disposables, getting rid of his dated glasses.

After dinner, we paid and went home. Will left the next day and from then on I was conscious that every word was listened to; even when we made love there would be someone listening – but that was just a way of life for us and something I had to accept in the man and the relationship I had chosen.

Yes, I was scared; I was totally out of my league and that's frightening, but it felt good to be with him and I had total trust in his ability to protect us. It felt good to be loved so much by someone who was making a difference to the world. I didn't and don't think of myself as overly special, but I felt that I was special to him.

4

A Miracle

May 2001

By May 2001 it felt like we had known each other a lifetime, although he'd had to move base because of my visit to Gullane. It was announced in *The Times* that he had been appointed as an IT director to a big company in Manchester, and he spent more and more time down there. We did see each other on weekends, though, and usually got to spend at least one night a week together. He promised me that it would only be for a short time and that things would change very soon.

I started to plan for the future, having formally accepted Will's marriage proposal after he spoke to my father in February, and organised an engagement party to celebrate with all my family and friends. Unfortunately, however, the intended groom didn't turn up. He was obviously supposed to be there and had gone to London to pick up his parents, who had travelled over especially for the occasion. But they'd had a massive falling out because he'd made a comment about his mother's shoes, and his parents had thought he was ashamed of them. Will was deeply embarrassed about the incident, particularly as the row had escalated to the point where his parents just got back on the plane and returned to the US without coming up to Edinburgh. In fact, Will was so mortified that he couldn't face coming to Edinburgh either, but just immersed himself in a rather feeble mission for the service that could have been avoided in favour of his engagement party. Afterwards he was deeply remorseful and apologetic.

His mother got in touch with me via email and was extremely diplomatic about the incident, simply saying that she regretted not being able to be there. We had emailed each other several times already, but it was difficult to keep a conversation going with her as she would forget what we had written before. Will had already warned me about his mother being quite seriously ill, suffering from bipolar manic depression from around the time he was born. This was something we had in common, as I had experience of the condition through my own family. I knew that his mother was particularly badly affected and had had to be hospitalised several times. His father was a wonderful man, constantly looking after his wife and standing by her side. As they were both retired, finances were tough, particularly when there were hospital bills to pay, but generally they were happy. Will's dad knew about Will's career in the intelligence service but he was the only member of his family who did. His mother was not stable enough to handle the information and his sister was not included either; they just thought that he was a bad communicator who was busy with his work.

I spoke to his parents on the telephone only once and they were friendly and open, enthusiastic about Will being part of a family at last, especially since he could not have his own children. It was an international conference call, with both his mother and father on the line at the same time, and his mother talked to me about learning French and wanting to go to Paris. I was very excited to speak to them, but even though we promised to keep in touch by phone, and I often saw Will chatting to them, I never spoke to them again. I asked him to let me say hello, but it just never seemed convenient at the time.

◆ ◆ ◆

Sometime in the spring of 2001, I noticed one hair on Will's chest. I teased him about it mercilessly. It was a single solid-black hair growing out of his chest, just left of the centre. He laughed about it and protected it when I threatened to pluck it out. It was quite extraordinary and we wondered at the time why it had happened. Will was baffled and could offer no explanation at all, though he was clearly quite boyishly proud about it. Later, more came and gradually over the next few years he produced a whole chest of hair. He also started to grow facial hair and had to shave around once a week, later more often.

The next development was even more astounding. In June 2001, we were busy preparing for our wedding in July when I discovered I was pregnant. I was terrified he would think I had been unfaithful (which I had not), as he had been so sure about his inability to father a child. I got him to come home from work in Manchester and told him the news. He turned white with shock and I thought he was going to pass out; he had to lean against the wall to support himself. He was stunned, then elated, calling me magic and a witch. He said it was a miracle, that the doctors had said it was possible but very, very unlikely. My fears were unfounded. He was overjoyed and swept me into his arms. If possible, he became even more affectionate and attentive than before, always touching and cuddling me. He kept repeating, 'They always said it was a remote possibility; I just never thought it could actually happen!'

As I had already told my family about his infertility, they were stunned to hear I was pregnant. They kept asking how this could be possible, and I could only tell them what Will had told me: that all the tests had indicated he was infertile and we had no idea how we had managed to conceive a child together.

The wedding venue was booked, the dress had been bought and taken out due to my expanding waistline, and invitations were being issued, when Will vanished again. He was gone for two weeks before I was contacted through 'MOD RELAY' with a message that said he was alive and well and would be in touch when he could. The wedding was cancelled. I had to face people with no explanation other than that work had intervened. 'No matter, we'll do it later,' I told everyone.

My family and friends were pretty aggressive about Will missing his wedding due to work commitments. They were very protective towards me but I wouldn't let them put him down. I supported his actions and refused to allow people to say anything bad about him. After all, I knew the reasons; I just couldn't explain them, and so my friends and family just had to accept that. I did a very good job of putting a bright and happy face on it and tried to show everyone that I was OK so they wouldn't worry – it was the only thing I could do.

Will was away from July 2001 to May 2002, apart from a twenty-four-hour stopover in December 2001. He explained that he was out in Israel and the West Bank working with Israeli intelligence to keep ahead of the suicide bombers. He had managed to score this brief trip home to replace broken equipment, but he would be heading straight back out again the next day. We had a blessed and wonderful day and night where he touched and talked to my swollen belly and told me how much he loved and missed me. He held me and loved me, and we were both torn apart when he had to leave.

One of the worst parts of it was that he was unable to provide for us financially while he was away and, with no child support for my first daughter either, I had to manage on my own. Will had no access to funds and had not managed to set up anything before he went. In fact, they'd had to leave so fast that the company he had set up in Edinburgh had gone bust and Donna – one of his employees – didn't get paid her last month's salary. She rang me a couple of times and asked if I knew where he was, but I could not tell her anything.

Luckily I was still working, but it was difficult to make ends meet with one child in full-time nursery and another on the way. I was really worried about taking maternity leave and wasn't sure how I would cope, but hopefully Will would be home by then.

I got a few phone calls from him and one in particular sticks out in my mind. I remember clearly because I was at work, watching the second plane crash into the Twin Towers on the live broadcast. I got a crackly and remote-sounding phone call from him to let me know he was OK. Because in theory no partners knew where their other halves were, the service allowed everyone to call home so their families would know they were safe. It was good to hear his voice and be reassured during such a devastating event.

However, most of the year we talked on MSN, where he'd tell me about the war zone he was in and what hell it was, particularly because of the suffocating heat. It was a frustrating way to communicate, especially as we would often be interrupted by what he described as 'interference', and our conversations had to take place between midnight and 5 a.m. I kept my computer volume turned up so that I could hear if he came online, and would sleep only lightly, given that I could be woken several times in the night by a crying child or by a computer alert saying there was a possibility of some news to reassure me that he was still alive. He frequently dangled the possibility that he might be able to make another trip home, but he never came, and I spent the whole of my pregnancy alone and afraid for his life.

My family were annoyed and pretty scathing about his absence. They asked me how he could stay away and said it was irresponsible of him. Every time they attacked him I felt I had to defend him, though I couldn't tell them where he really was and what he was doing.

I felt so protective towards him, especially when he sent me pictures of the devastation and told me how he and the team had had to get to bomb sites before the press to assess the situation while the victims were still in situ. It was his job and I didn't want to hassle him too much about it; after all, I had a roof over my head as well as heat, light and water. I was not living in fear of being killed at any moment. It was selfish of me to complain at all, as, at the end of the day, everything is relative.

Will was adamant that, even though he was still overseas, he had made arrangements to ensure that he'd be home for the birth of his baby.

◆ ◆ ◆

Eilidh was born in February 2002, with my mother by my side. As soon as I went into labour, I emailed Will and he emailed back saying he was on his way and would come straight to the hospital.

The birth was exciting, to say the least. The cord was wrapped around the baby's chest and her heart was slowing down almost to a stop with each contraction. The midwife broke my waters and put an electrode on to the baby's scalp via the birth canal to get a better reading, and more people were called into the room.

My mother held my hand as I panted on the gas. She looked terrified and was squeezing my hand hard. More staff came in and there were eventually two doctors and three midwives in the room. Everyone was telling me not to push, so I concentrated hard, trying my best to follow their instructions. Then they took away my precious gas and air, replacing it with an oxygen mask. Eventually they decided that I would need an immediate Caesarean section and started to unhook all the wires to move me through to the operating theatre, but I took the mask off and said I wanted to push. At that point they said I could if I wanted, and Eilidh was born naturally three minutes later.

I had never felt closer to my mother than I did that day and was so glad she had been there with me. I could tell that she was pretty upset with Will for failing to show up, but she didn't say very much as she didn't want to upset me. By that stage she knew that if she attacked him I would only defend him, and that would push me closer to him.

When I was finally left alone with my baby, I lay looking at her for hours. She slept and slept, looking so much like her daddy. Every time the door to the ward opened, I looked up with a surge of hope, expecting to see Will come in. He did not appear, and with each disappointment my spirits sank further and I felt more alone. Other fathers arrived and sat by their partners' beds, held their babies and cried. I waited and hoped, but Will did not come.

He found out that I had given birth to a daughter when I arrived home the next day and emailed him. I hadn't heard from him since I went into labour and I was starting to worry, as he had been so adamant that he would make it back in time for the birth. It was several days later that I finally received a reply, saying how proud he was to be a father and that he was so very sorry not to have been there. He asked me to send photographs so he could see the baby and told me again that he was on his way and would be there to help soon.

5

BACK FROM THE MASSACRE

May 2002

When Will did finally appear in May 2002, he was haggard and thin, crippled from wearing his boots for three months solid. He and his team had been dropped into the Palestinian town of Jenin for a twenty-four-hour reconnaissance mission. They were supposed to be just in and out, but then Israeli troops moved into the area and they had been trapped in the massacre. Knowing Will was out there, I had followed the news of the Israeli/Palestinian conflict with passionate interest the whole time he was away. I knew everything the press had reported about the massacre already, but had not known Will was actually there. He told me about the madness of it all: how the Israelis had gone street by street, bulldozing civilians within their own homes and killing indiscriminately. Soldiers and even officers who had refused to carry out the atrocities had apparently been shot by more senior staff – and the rest had done as they were told.

Will and the other members of his team had survived in the rubble with little equipment or supplies and had had to eat rats to survive. The trick is, apparently, to catch them before you get too hungry to chase them.

When they were finally picked up by their support, Will had to have his socks surgically removed from his feet by medical staff and spent two weeks in hospital. He was very shy about showing me his feet and refused to take his socks off in bed. I did see them when he showered, however, and they were in a dreadful state. The skin was broken and raw, but was now starting to heal over. After his stint in hospital, he had spent even more time in debriefing before being sent home. But it was over. They were unlikely to be sent back again soon.

It was hard to complain about being stood up, even for the birth of a child, when faced with that explanation for his absence. My disappointment and loneliness seemed pretty petty by comparison and I was just relieved to have him back. I had worried about him so much when he was away and had existed in a state of constant stress, carrying my mobile phone with me every minute of the day in case he needed or was able to contact me.

When he walked through the door, however, and I knew he was safe, suddenly everything was all right again. All my worries dissipated and were replaced by a surge of relief and love. He had come home for us, just as he had promised. Like a smoker who has been deprived of a cigarette for a long time forgets all the hours of suffering and withdrawal when they take their first drag, my joy at seeing him alive and well, and feeling our family whole again, wiped away my annoyance at the broken promises and frustration at his absence.

This was the pattern that we established and which I fell into each time he came back to us. I saw him so little that I wanted to make the most of my time with him rather than spoil it with arguments and angst. I wanted him to enjoy being home; after all, he had suffered much more than me while we had been apart.

When he finally met Eilidh for the first time, he seemed stunned. He cradled her and put his finger in her hand, letting her grip curl around it. She looked bemused by him and was clearly not sure of this stranger, but she relaxed quickly as he made faces and noises for her. He looked smitten, and even though he was exhausted and ill he loved being a daddy at last – something he had believed impossible.

But despite his joy at being home and meeting his daughter, Will was clearly depressed. He had become disillusioned with his work and had lost faith in the service and what it was fighting for. He had believed in what he'd spent his life doing up until then, but now it all seemed futile and hypocritical. The massacre in Jenin had shown him there was fault on both sides, and he had sympathy for Palestinians who felt that the only means of keeping their plight in the world's eye was to strap a bomb to themselves and detonate it after walking into a crowded area. Will felt that the CIA weren't achieving anything out there. There was no solution and no one was right. He felt he had done his bit and now he wanted to be home with his family. He wanted out, and I supported his decision to resign from the service. But extracting himself from the CIA would prove anything but easy.

Will was very busy with debriefing over the next few months. There were several meetings with the team about how to deal with the aftermath of the Jenin massacre and he had to keep coming and going, though we did see quite a bit of him over the summer. But leaving the CIA was not like resigning from a normal job. They were certainly not keen to let him go and were determined to keep him on in whatever capacity they could. After all, they had spent a lot of time and money training him and they did not want that investment to be wasted.

One day, Will came home excited about the consultancy work they had offered him – it had been put to him that this was almost equivalent to a promotion to management. This was the compromise: they accepted his retirement from active service but he was not 'out' altogether. Initially the consultancy work would mean training other officers in surveillance and information gathering, but he would also be providing them with his contacts and expertise. I would have preferred him to walk away from it all, but Will obviously felt he could not cut ties with his life's work as easily as that.

His retirement from active service had an immediate financial impact on us, as he lost all the perks such as the cars and cash card. This was a blow to Will; he'd worked all his life, but he now had nothing to show for it. Personally, I didn't care about the loss of money or possessions; in fact, I had seen very little of this anyway. I just wanted my fiancé and the father of my child by my side. I wanted to support him through this difficult transition and help him bond with his family once again.

For a while, Will was around more, for weekends and days at a time. Robyn and Eilidh adored him and it started to feel like we were a proper family, though Will was still depressed and seemed physically weak, so he did not play with the children much. He talked all the time about how much he loved them, but was quite reserved and a little formal in their company –almost as if he felt shy around them. I felt it was simply because spending time with kids was new to him and he needed to get used to them, so I encouraged him to engage with them more. We invented physical games like the 'sack game', in which he would carry them around in a blanket like Santa Claus and his sack, and the children loved it. They particularly liked climbing on Will and getting piggyback rides; one day we went to numerous shops to buy lots and lots of building blocks so that we could build a huge castle together. Left to his own devices, though, Will would slip away and go back to working on his computer.

He was still wonderful and made an effort to be part of the family: he would clean the house and hoover when home, and even cook – though I suspect that was largely because he preferred his own cooking to my culinary efforts.

In October 2002, we set a new date to get married. This time it would be kept quiet and be a very small affair, mostly to keep it from his employer, as by this time I was convinced they were actively trying to separate us. It seemed that every time we planned something as a family, Will would be called away, and always at the most inopportune moments. Will told me that they were not pleased he was having a relationship outside the service – something that rarely happened – because it took his attention away from his work. Prior to our relationship, he had been a 100 per cent theirs.

I also did not want to face family and friends again if another wedding failed to occur, so we set the date for 26 October and I waited to see if he'd arrive in time. He came home on the twenty-fifth and we spent the evening drinking champagne and eating pizza. He was here; this was really happening!

The day of our wedding dawned and he was still there. I was elated and finally allowed myself to get excited about it. We called the witness, a lovely friend of mine called Kezza, who was the only person we'd told in advance. Kezza was so excited for me that she had been up since 6 a.m. waiting for the call to say it was going ahead – I could hear her physically jumping up and down when I told her he was here, and this fuelled my own excitement for the day.

Then I called my family to say, 'We're getting married today if you'd like to come.' By this time they were used to Will coming and going. Although they were happy for me because I was happy, they were also quite wary of him. They had picked up the not-so-vague hints I had offered about his profession, but it had not been discussed all that openly. I would tell them that there was more to it than I could say, and then change the subject when they tried to pursue the conversation. They had been pretty cynical about our relationship, but I think the fact that we were finally getting married convinced them that he was genuine about me.

The day of our wedding was wonderful. It was a lovely way to get married. There were no flowers, or cars, or photographers, or guest seating plans, or stresses and politics. Just us. Just our commitment and promise to each other.

We dressed separately and I put on a coat to hide my simple white lace, low-cut cocktail dress. Then we told the babysitter we were off to get married. We jumped in a cab and asked the driver to take us to Victoria Street Registry Office, via Rose Street, because we had to buy a ring for Will. Mine had already been bought, but Will had not been around for his to be sized. When we walked into the shop, the assistants were calm and professional. They asked when the wedding was and when we looked at our watches and said, 'In thirty-one minutes', they both went into shocked overdrive. Every ring was brought out at top speed to find one that fitted, but Will was adamant he wanted the one that matched mine. He was always like that, wanting matching coats and things that would remind him of me when he was away. However, the matching ring they had in the shop was a couple of sizes too big. As a compromise, we agreed he'd use it for the ceremony but order the correct size and exchange it at a later date. We then ran back to the car and sped off to the registry office.

My father and mother were there waiting for us. My mother was not entirely comfortable with the whole situation, although she was glad we were marrying and that Will was making a firm commitment to the kids and me. My sister Isobel then appeared with her whole family. She was excited that it was finally happening and was very bubbly. She acted as Will's best man while breastfeeding her own baby throughout the service to keep him quiet. The joke, of course, was that she was his 'breast man'.

My six-foot-four brother arrived looking like something out of a horror movie. He'd played rugby the day before and the white of one of his eyes was completely red due to a burst blood vessel. He appeared wearing dark glasses and my mother said, 'Take them off, Neil', which he did without speaking; then she looked at him and just said, 'Put them back on again', which again he did without uttering a word, making us all laugh out loud.

I found myself nervous before the ceremony, although there was no shred of doubt in my mind about marrying Will. Will, as always, was calm personified and showed no nerves at all, happy to be finally getting married. The ceremony was intense and personal. We made our lifelong commitment to each other and only each other, a commitment to stand by each other, to be honest and true, faithful and loyal. Now and forever, and no matter what.

'I do solemnly declare that I know not of any lawful impediment why I, William Allen Jordan, may not be joined in matrimony to Mary Turner Thomson.'

I made my vow, surprised at how difficult it was to remember the actual words when you are standing there saying them yourself. Then it was his turn, and I looked deep into his loving eyes as he stood and repeated the intense and binding words to me with passion and love.

'I take you, Mary Turner Thomson, to be my lawful wedded wife, to have and to hold from this day forward, for better or for worse, for richer, for poorer, in sickness and in health, to love and to cherish, from this day forward until death do us part.'

They are words you often hear – at friends' weddings, on television and in films – but when you say them yourself as a binding vow in front of witnesses, they take on new meaning and power. The words are a solid commitment to another person to stand by them, through everything, to make it work no matter what, for a lifetime. It was a commitment that I believed in and valued.

After we'd signed the marriage contract, we went for lunch at the Tron, a converted church just below Edinburgh Castle, and then my brother took Will and me up to the Camera Obscura to look at the whole city. Afterwards, we went home to play with the kids and had some time together as a family. That evening, my mother held a dinner party for us, attended by those who had been at the wedding. We drank champagne and celebrated, my family pulling together and my husband by my side. I felt on top of the world. It was the happiest day of my life.

After the wedding, Will started doing more practical contract work for the CIA within the UK. He did a lot of driving for visiting dignitaries who required specialist and confidential transport: that is, they needed a secure driver who could act as a bodyguard and who was security checked.

Then in late 2002, Will's mother went into hospital and he was desperate to help. His father was unable to pay the hospital bill and Will needed to raise £5,000 to send to the US. We discussed it and agreed that I would raise a loan for £7,500, which meant I could also put £2,500 towards the overdraft I had built up. I gave £5,000 in cash to Will so that he could get it transferred to his father.

I was also becoming financially committed to him in other ways. At one point, Will needed to get a car quickly for a driving contract, as the ODCI could not provide one. It could not be in his name, because then it could possibly be traced back to Edinburgh and to us, so he persuaded me to hire it for him. I did not really understand why he needed it, even though he explained it several times, and I was uncomfortable with the situation because it was not legal. He was adamant that it was necessary, however, and promised that it would only be for a couple of days. It turned out to be for several months and almost my entire salary went on it. Will

54

did come home throughout that time but just kept saying that he needed the car for another few days. He repeatedly promised that he was about to return it, but did not actually bring it back until I threw a complete wobbler and threatened to call the police.

Will was now working all hours but not getting paid – a situation he was never able to explain to my satisfaction. I sank further and further into debt, but because I had such a good credit rating my overdraft was simply enlarged each month; it got to £7,000 before the bank drew a line under it. This was unfamiliar territory for me but I tried not to worry too much, as Will was constantly telling me that our financial situation was about to change.

We certainly needed a break, as our living situation was far from ideal. Space was tight in the flat, as we had two bedrooms that the children slept in while we shared a sofa bed in the living room. Despite our money problems, we started to discuss buying a larger property together. We believed this would be possible because Will and his team were due a massive payout from the Jenin mission, mostly to keep quiet about it – particularly about the massacre. The whole situation had blown up in the press and I read about the UN fact-finding team that had been sent out to discover the truth. Although the Israelis had agreed to their visit, they were turned away by the Israeli forces at the last minute, and then there was no more coverage. The story just fizzled out. Will was personally supposed to receive £250,000 compensation and with this, as well as the money from the sale of the house his aunt had left him in the US, we should have had enough to buy a new home.

Will showed me his Bank of America online account that had around $350,000 in it from the house sale, with more due. His father had access to the account and Will said he would get the money forwarded over after they had paid the tax on the sale. After all our problems, I really believed that we'd turned a corner.

In the first quarter of 2003, we therefore started house hunting and I found a wonderful flat in Bruntsfield in Edinburgh. We loved it and asked the owner what it would cost to take it off the market. He said £450,000. Will said, 'Done', without any hesitation at all. We completed the paperwork and the day came to transfer the money, but Will had vanished again. He promised daily that the money from the US was coming – there was a hiccup, a delay, 'This afternoon it'll all be sorted' – but it didn't arrive.

Eventually I had to pull the plug. Desperate and crushingly embarrassed, I had to tell the vendors to put the flat back on the market. They did, and luckily sold it for a good deal more than we'd offered; however, they charged us for the costs of reselling and the whole episode cost us £17,000.

Will did eventually turn up again days after I'd had to back-track on the sale of the flat, and explained that once again the service had tripped us up. The tax authorities had seized his bank account for the income tax payable on the sale of his US property and were processing what was due. Will told me that it was clear the CIA were pulling strings behind the scenes and were preventing the funds from being released, though he could not explain clearly to me why they would do this. The tax authorities would hold all funds until the situation was resolved, and then release the rest. He did not know when, but assured me it would happen 'soon'.

I thought this was all part of a concerted attempt to stop him getting out of the service completely. It seemed that his colleagues were not happy about his decision to leave, because they were like a family and saw it as a betrayal. He was letting them down by choosing the kids and me instead of doing his duty and continuing to serve his country. It was understandable that they were making life difficult for him – they were using him as an example to deter others from following suit.

6

THE HONEYMOON

February 2003

Will's depression continued, and he was struggling with life in general. Having lost his vocation and calling but still tied into the service, he started to resent what he had to do, and started to hate being called away. He was thin and haggard and generally down.

In February 2003, we decided to take a trip to London, something we did occasionally. Will had managed to get VIP tickets to *Phantom of the Opera* which he was very keen to see, including a special pre-show champagne event. My mother agreed to look after the children and we headed off in the afternoon.

We drove down from Edinburgh to London in record time and talked all the way. Will told me more about the horror he'd lived through and some of the stuff he'd seen. He talked about seeing the bloodshed, the bodies of children lying in the streets and how futile it all was. He talked again about the suicide bombers and how the Palestinian people had no other way to keep their plight in the public eye. I was fascinated listening to him, as it filled in some of the blanks and explained his depression.

Shortly before this trip, a friend of Will's, a man in the Israeli intelligence service called Avi, had been killed by a suicide bomb in Israel. Even though Will was clearly upset by his friend's death, he managed to pull himself out of his distress to put on a brave face for my family at an evening dinner party. At the time, I was amazed at his self-control and ability to laugh and joke and pretend he was fine – but then, that was all part of his job.

We did not arrive in time to go to the theatre that evening, mostly because we got lost driving through London. Will was annoyed with himself for not getting there, but I kept chirpy and said it was fun just to spend time together. We went to the hotel and had a romantic evening alone instead.

In the morning, we wandered around holding hands and shopping. He took me to various electronic shops, and to one in particular that had a whole section of surveillance equipment. There were cameras that could be put in light bulbs and ordinary clock radios with sound receivers in them.

He clearly knew his way around and pointed out specific items, talking all the time about surveillance and how it worked. He told me how to look out for things and how to spot something odd. I found this fascinating but knew they were things I'd never detect – for instance, he showed me a working electrical socket with a hole where a camera could be placed instead of a screw, and a smoke detector that was actually a camera and sound-bugging device. The best devices were ones that had a direct power source, because battery power did not last that long. Pens and packets of cigarettes might be fancy, but they had a short life in surveillance terms.

'If in doubt,' he said, 'just always assume you are bugged and then you'll be safe.' He said the most effective surveillance device was usually a clock, because it was often placed where it could be seen from all angles, meaning in turn that it could 'see' every part of the room. He showed me how there was usually a small black dot, a hole in the number twelve, through which the camera could see all. In this particular shop, there was every kind of clock conceivable.

'This makes it easier and quicker,' he said, 'just to get in and see what kind of clock they have, then go back and replace it with the surveillance model.'

It was an amazing place, an Aladdin's cave of camera pens and gadgets for the average, or not-so-average, spook. Will said that often it was quicker to buy things himself than wait for the service to issue stuff, and the equipment available on the commercial market was now as good and often better than what the service supplied.

That night we went out to dinner and got tickets for *Les Misérables*. It was a production I had already seen and absolutely loved. However, Will had not seen it before and the effect on him was astounding. He was devastated.

We had to drive straight back to Edinburgh overnight after the performance, and he could not speak to me the whole way. It was the first and only time that his driving worried me, as I could not tell if he was even alert or not. He would not say what was wrong, just muttering one-word grunts and mumbles. It scared the hell out of me as I sat trying to work out what could have affected him so badly. Was it that the musical told the story of a rehabilitated convict? Will had told me early on in our relationship that he had once been in prison: when he was only eighteen, he was arrested for writing less than a hundred dollars' worth of bad cheques. His mother had once again been in hospital, and he'd had to find a way to get food for his sister. Will had known there was not enough money in the family account to cover the cheques, but he was desperate. He told me that his defence was hampered by the judge's perception that a black teenage boy was just trying to cheat the system, so he was imprisoned for a couple of months to teach him a lesson.

I wondered if the musical had reminded him of this horrible time, but then came to the conclusion that it must be more complex than that. Perhaps the images of the revolution and the students fighting a futile war against the organised government forces brought back the horror he had witnessed in Jenin. Certainly I had never seen him in that state before; it was like watching the ground I was standing on crumble away beneath me.

Worried about his mental state, over the next three months I tried to go easy on Will. He continued to come and go, and sometimes disappeared for two or three weeks at a stretch. I felt desperately lonely and isolated but tried to remain strong for him. He told me that he was working on IT contracts again and I did not ask him too many questions. I did not want to put further pressure on him and be responsible for pushing him over the edge. On several occasions, he said he'd put £5,000 into my bank account 'over the counter', but it did not appear. When I queried it, he swore that it had been done and said he'd get on to the bank. This happened several times and I started to wonder if this was a symptom of a breakdown – that he was lying as he couldn't handle the truth that there was no money.

In May 2003, Will came home quite often and we started to play chess together, something both of us were relatively good at. We would order a pizza, open a bottle of wine and relax. Will would usually beat me, but when I won he was equally happy about it. He was never competitive. But despite these moments of respite I remained concerned about his mental health, and our money worries continued to grow. He was not providing any financial support for me or the kids and I was struggling to keep the family afloat. My sleep patterns suffered due to stress and also because I would often be up late at night talking to Will via MSN or email. I started to show physical symptoms, getting multiple ulcers in my mouth and even on my eyes. I had to visit the hospital on several occasions and ended up wearing an eye patch for a while to cure a particularly nasty ulcer on my right cornea. The doctors told me it was directly related to stress and asked if I was sleeping, to which I always just replied that I was.

I continued to work at my job, advising businesses, and had also started to run school programmes, teaching a two- or three-day practical business start-up course to large groups of fifteen- and sixteen-year-olds. I also started doing more and more training courses for business people for the Chamber of Commerce, teaching motivation, PR, advertising, starting a business and marketing. I found I loved training people and that I was a good motivator, whatever course I was teaching. I started working extra hours at my job, agreeing to man the office on a Saturday morning to earn more money. My mother made this possible by agreeing to have the girls each week, so it would be additional income without additional childcare costs.

I always missed Will so much when he was away; I tried hard just to get on with life and put on a brave face, although I was scared all the time. Raising two small children on your own is not easy at the best of times, but while lonely and in fear for your husband's life, and constantly on guard to protect your family from 'unsavouries', it is harrowing. I was like an army wife, but without the network of support that army wives have around them. I loved my two little girls and knew that my stress levels must be affecting them, though I tried hard not to show it, even to them.

As our first anniversary approached in October 2003, we decided that we would have a honeymoon, and on request from Will I looked for a hotel with a four-poster bed and what he called a 'bubble-tub' in the room. I found the perfect place in the out-of-the-way, luxurious Shieldhill Castle, and we made a reservation for three nights.

As always, Will was cutting it fine. He texted to say he was on the train and I went to Waverley Station in Edinburgh to meet him. I met every train until they stopped for the night, then sat in the car. I could not go home as it would disturb the kids, and I also could not face the embarrassment of having been stood up again.

I understood. It meant that Will's phone was being monitored and he wanted someone else to think he was on a train. It still upset me, though. He did call to say he was still coming and that I should go to the hotel and he'd meet me there. It was too late by then, so I got a room in a Holiday Inn and went the next morning instead.

Shieldhill Castle is stunning and just the most romantic of places, surrounded by beautiful grounds. It's an intimate hotel and the place was not full. In fact, the only other guests were a German family and a BBC crew who were filming a socialist politician taking the place of the laird for a week to see how the other half live.

I arrived and settled in, had a bath and sat on the amazing four-poster bed. Wow, what a room! But there was no sign of Will, and by this stage I did not expect him to show up. I figured I would stay for one night then head off home, so I went down to dinner. The BBC crew were sitting at one large table in the middle of the restaurant and the staff seated me at a small table by the window right next to them.

It must have been an odd sight, a woman sitting alone in such a romantic retreat, so they started talking to me and asked what I was doing there.

'I'm on my honeymoon,' I said.

Astonished, they asked where my husband was.

'Beats me,' I commented.

For the first time, I made no attempt to defend him or come up with a story or answer that fitted. Instead, I steered the conversation away from myself and my absent husband as smoothly as three years of practice could allow. I talked to them about the programme they were making and drank a bottle of wine on my own. I used to work for the BBC back in 1987. I had worked in the studios at Television Centre on *EastEnders* and *All Creatures Great and Small* as an assistant floor manager, so there were areas we had in common. I didn't join their table but remained in my own romantic position, resolutely enjoying the experience alone. Actually, the waitress helped a great deal by tripping over the champagne cooler that she had placed beside my table. The bottle and a whole bucket of ice went flying across the floor. She was mortified, but I was glad that the commotion had distracted attention from me. Afterwards, I headed to the bar and stood drinking whiskies with the laird and his son, cracking jokes and enjoying their company – I was determined that I would enjoy myself regardless.

Will did arrive later that night, around midnight. He came up to the room with a bottle of champagne and did not even apologise. Well, why should he, when he had been working for the government and it was not his choice to be held up? Like the wife of a doctor on call, I should know the priorities by now.

We had a wonderful, sexy, romantic few days. Will did use his laptop a bit and contacted work a few times, but mostly he left it alone and relaxed. We walked in the country and around the chapel; we threw sticks for the castle's spaniels; we walked into the town and had tea; and we had scones with jam and cream in the Oak Room Lounge. The food was wonderful, the staff friendly and accommodating, and the wine flowed.

We revelled in each other's company. Always gentle and attentive, Will made it a memorable honeymoon, making me feel loved and valued and adored. We bathed together numerous times in the Jacuzzi with glasses of bubbly in our hands, laughing and sharing anecdotes. Then we would lie naked on the bed watching DVDs and drinking more champagne. We made love again and again, and felt connected once more, our partnership revitalised and strengthened.

Will was very nervous about the camera crew being there. Obviously, because of his profession, it was important that he did not appear on television, and he was uncomfortable about the idea of them getting footage of him. As we were leaving, they asked if they could film us paying, but Will declined. They asked me if I would do it on my own, and I reluctantly agreed. I have a passionate dislike of being on camera, specifically television or video, but an equally strong compulsion to be helpful and do as I am asked. So I paid for the room and board while a whole BBC crew watched, with Will behind them grinning at me. My performance was not aired.

The whole holiday (apart from being on camera) was, and is, a lovely memory.

7

NEW JOB, NEW HOUSE, NEW LIFE

November 2003

Will decided that the only way he could get out of the service completely was to set up a business that was untainted by anything the CIA did. To do this, he'd have to ensure nothing was in his name and nothing was traceable back to him. So, he organised for a limited company to be set up with me as the managing director. Everything would be in my name, including the bank account and so on. I had to sign forms and register for VAT, but the business was really Will's. He was in control, did the VAT returns and told me what to do with the money. I was still working and, although a confident adviser in marketing and business, I was never financially minded, so Will would take care of everything on that side of things. He had a plan and I trusted my husband implicitly to know what he was doing. I was convinced this was the only way forward and enjoyed the title, albeit in name only.

He soon got a contract working as an IT programmer for a large software company in Cambridge, working on a specific aspect of their multimedia software. He would fax me his timesheets and I would put the invoice together as he requested and fax it on to the agents for payment. Suddenly money started to come in and life changed, as he had always promised it would. He was bringing in between £6,000 and £10,000 per month, and now we could afford to pay the bills. On Christmas Eve, we went together to look at cars for me to use, and bought one on hire purchase based on the income he was bringing into the business in my name. This was the first time I had ever even driven a new car, and it felt wonderful. It felt like we were on the way up.

The only problem was that Will was away most of the time, working on the contract in Cambridge. He tended to come home most weekends and we talked on the phone daily and were on MSN almost constantly. I hated that he had to work away and asked him frequently to find clients in Edinburgh, but he reminded me that this was the nature of IT contract work.

Will did manage to be home for Christmas Day itself, though – the first he had actually succeeded in spending with us, and it was lovely to wake up on Christmas morning with him. The children and I had always stayed over at my mother's and father's house so that we could enjoy the day with my parents, so we did the same that year and were joined later on by my sister Isobel and her family, as well as my brother. There was a frenzy of present-opening followed by a wonderful meal cooked, as always, by my mum. Then came the traditional game of charades, which we all enjoyed. It felt so nice to be together and feel like a proper family. The children were really happy that Will was there, and finally his promises were starting to come true. We were spending more time together and starting to live the lifestyle he had always wanted for us.

With Christmas over, we started to look to the future. Things were still very cramped in my two-bedroom flat, especially as the children started to move around more and take up more space. Now we had the money, Will suggested that we move. However, I was not keen to repeat the house-buying experience, and so Will suggested that we rent a house until we had managed to sort out his money from the US, saving his earnings in the meantime to build up more capital.

So, at the tail end of December 2003, we moved into a rented four-bedroom house in south Edinburgh, which was lovely. The house had been built over a filled-in quarry and had settled. It was, therefore, as squint as it's possible for a house to be without actually falling over. If you dropped a marble at the front door, it would roll down the corridor, make a left turn, then a right turn, into the kitchen and then out the back door. We were assured that it was not going to settle any more, but it took me a long time to get used to the crookedness of it – when I had guests round, they said it felt better after a few glasses of wine.

The house had a dining room, kitchen with utility room off it, front room, playroom and shower room downstairs, along with four bedrooms and a bathroom upstairs. It had gardens front and back and decking in front of the shed. It gave us enough room to breathe and to expand, and I loved living that lifestyle. I had space to put out things my grandmother had given me and to have a grown-up living room as well as a dedicated playroom for the children. More importantly, though, it was in the right catchment area for the school I wanted Robyn to go to, which she would start at that summer.

My parents had bought a wonderful big house in the same area when I was ten years old, less than two blocks from this house, and it felt like coming home. It felt right, albeit squint. The rent was £1,700 per month but that was perfectly possible on the income Will was now earning. I rented out my own flat to a friend who was a single mother, and because she was short of cash I did not hassle her if she did not make the rent. In the scheme of things, it was not much money and it was a way of keeping the flat and a step on the property ladder.

We used one of the main bedrooms as an office for the two of us and set up two desks and printers, a fax machine and so on. It finally felt like all my patience was paying off. I loved it when Will was home and we would sit working together – me on marketing or business reports and him on website designs or his software company contract work. Having an office at home allowed me to work from there, and gave me much more freedom with my working hours.

Will spent the first half of 2004 buying computer equipment – he had set a budget of £10,000 through the business to do this. Technology and web design were taking off and the Internet was becoming the major means of global communication. It had been just over ten years since the World Wide Web became publicly available but it had already changed the world as we knew it. He bought servers on eBay, along with battery-run back-up units and hard drives – all equipment that (even though I had quite a good grasp of technology) was beyond my technical knowhow. By May 2004, there were two waist-height stacked towers of noisy, fan-driven, electronic web-hosting, kick-ass servers taking over a good portion of our dining room. My friends were seriously impressed and joked about his ability to run a small country from the house. I was not privy to what was run on the servers except Will's website-development work and the business emails that went through them.

Will put wireless broadband into the house so that we could work from any room, and the multimedia-software contract stuff he worked on was fabulous: TV through the PC, record-and-pause live TV and so on. It was fun to show people the stuff he had been doing and I was so proud of him. It all gave him the ability to do consultancy work for the ODCI and to set up websites for the business privately. Most importantly, however, it would help him strike out totally on his own and work from home, meaning that the family would be together more of the time, something he desperately wanted as much as me.

One day, Will came back all excited saying he'd found a wonderful car: could we go and see it? We duly did, and it was a huge Mercedes 4x4 with tinted windows. He was like a kid in a toyshop, hopping from foot to foot saying, 'Please can I have it, please?'

How could I say no? It was his money, even if it was going through my business account. He was over the moon and thanked me over and over. He said no one had ever done anything like this for him and it was the first time he really felt he had been given something outside his work. Again, the car had to be in my name and I didn't even blink this time, as I was getting used to the idea. While signing the finance agreement they asked if I wanted a credit card, too, as I was pre-approved. I was unsure; it was something I had avoided altogether until now because I was worried about getting into debt – I even sweated if I got a red bill! However, Will encouraged me to go ahead, saying it would make life a lot easier, so I did.

Will initially let me have around £3,000 per month out of his income to pay the rent and the car payments, which left me around £500 per month for bills and food. He organised for me to get another two credit cards and even applied for them online on my behalf. All in all, this was a good time, and seemed to be getting better.

The downside was that Will was working all hours, sleeping in the office or the car when he was at work so that he could save money and maximise the billable hours on his timesheet – indeed, he was doing around seventy-two hours a week at this stage.

Then things started to get really difficult again. The contract in Cambridge started to suffer because Will kept vanishing, as the service were once again trying to pull him out of our life together. Then he told me that he had come across someone from a previous

CIA assignment which had made it difficult for him to continue there without putting us at risk. This person could trace him back to us, and as the assignment had involved infiltrating terrorist organisations there was a serious threat of violent repercussions. If he was traced back to his home in Scotland and his real family, i.e. to people who really mattered to him, we could be used to manipulate him. We could be kidnapped or injured in revenge or to gain a hold over him.

I was terrified by this and I told him how scared I was, particularly as he was not around to protect us if we were found. He said that I could be issued with a weapon to defend myself and the kids, but I refused in no uncertain terms.

'OK, how about a taser then?' he asked.

'What's a taser?' I asked.

'I'll get you one issued,' he said.

Within forty-eight hours, the taser was delivered to the house in an unmarked brown paper package and Will put it together at his desk.

It was an object about the size of a mobile phone. It had a U-shaped top, and when you switched it on and pressed a button it zapped a bolt of electricity between the two points of the U. It was a very effective defensive weapon, and as long as the assailant did not have a pacemaker, all it would do was knock them out. It was only for use at close quarters, though – it didn't work at a distance. I knew that it was illegal in the UK, but it was being issued by the CIA for the protection of an employee's family and Will told me that it was all right and had been cleared. However, it was certainly not something to be brandished about, and was only to be used when I needed to defend myself.

Will arranged for a professional ODCI trainer to teach me how to use it, but at the last minute the session had to be cancelled for some reason, so Will trained me himself. He showed me how the

CIA are taught to use this defensive tool, holding it and zapping a bolt of electricity through someone's body to incapacitate them.

'If you hit a leg or arm it just deadens that part of their body; you have to get them in the torso, shoulder or neck to knock them out completely.'

He showed me how to hold an assailant and demonstrated how, as long as I could touch them with the points of the taser, I could defend myself and the kids. The good thing about the weapon was that even if you were holding the person when you zapped them, you did not get shocked.

I never had to use the taser but it did help to know it was just at hand. It didn't stop my constant nightmares, however, and I repeatedly dreamt about waking to find people in the house, trying to take us away: men going into the children's room and having to find a way to stop them. I did not sleep well at all, feeling that we were always in danger, but by now I was used to lack of sleep; it had become a way of life.

My waking fears were only stopped by the sheer confidence Will had in his own ability to protect us, even when he was not there. We were watched over and he would know if anything was not right. I was actually more scared of the CIA than the 'unsavouries', because I was by now convinced that they blamed me for Will's 'desertion' and wanted me out of the way. But Will said that if they had allowed anything to happen to us, he would do damage to the service. They believed that I had taken him away from them, but getting rid of us would not bring him back to them – quite the contrary, he assured me.

8

HOLIDAY OF DISCOVERY

June 2004

In June 2004, we went on our first and last holiday together as a family, to Center Parcs in Norfolk – the only seven-consecutive-day week that we spent together in four years! It seemed incredible that we'd had so little time together, but the promise was always there: things were always about to change. All he had to do was get out of the service and we'd be free to have a life together. Up until then, we'd had weekends and two or maybe four days together at a time. Sometimes he would be home every week for a few days with a promise of more, but he always went away again and almost always at a moment's notice.

The holiday was really needed. I had suffered a miscarriage a month earlier, which had highlighted the possibility that we could have another child. That possibility, however slim, gave hope to us both and, although saddened by our loss, we decided to actively try for another baby. The holiday was a new start for us, an opportunity to spend time with the children and reconfirm our love for each other. I desperately wanted to give Will the son he desired, to give his father the continuation of the family name that Will's infertility had denied him. I wanted to recreate the miracle that had happened with the conception of our daughter and to give my two lovely girls another sibling. Will had always wanted more children, but we had thought it impossible. The miscarriage reignited his desire for another baby, because he saw it as hope for the future. He was more passionate when making love than ever before, saying that the prospect of creating new life intensified his feelings and his orgasms.

The holiday was wonderful. Will came up to Edinburgh and we travelled together, then stayed in a chalet that backed on to a lake. There were tame ducks and deer that came to the back door looking for breadcrumbs and scraps – all sorts of wildlife, which thrilled the children. There were no cars and we cycled everywhere. We spent time wandering around as the perfect normal family, happy and loving. The girls were in seventh heaven as there were playgrounds everywhere and the swimming pool was a children's paradise. There was so much to do, not to mention having Daddy to jump on and cuddle. Both the girls adored him; although Robyn was not his genetic child, she thought of him as 'Daddy' because she'd known him since she was one year old.

Towards the end of the holiday, Will got called away for a few hours for a meeting to do with work. He swore he would be back, and as he left his bags, I assumed he was actually telling the truth this time. There was nothing I could do to stop him, so I just had to let him go.

While he was gone, I went through to the bedroom and there, sitting as plain as day on the immaculately made-up bed, was a simple gold band, a wedding ring, and not the one I had given him on our wedding day. The ring I had given him, being two sizes too big, had been lost about a month after I put it on his finger. (He never got round to going back to the Rose Street shop and ordering the correct size.)

I picked up the ring and stared at it. There were no markings on it. It was just a straightforward plain gold band, large enough for his ring finger. There was no indentation on the bed; it was perfectly straight and smooth – it looked as though the ring had been placed carefully on top of it rather than having been dropped or fallen out of a pocket.

I sat down on the bed feeling confused and empty with the ring in my hand. My mind was completely blank, totally numb, for how long I do not know. Then my brain was flooded with so many questions and details that I could not comprehend or grasp anything.

My first conscious thought was that I was staring at Will's treasured brown bag on the floor by the bed. This was his battered leather document bag that he took with him everywhere, the bag in which he had stored the gun when he used to carry one, and which he locked in my cupboard when he visited my flat. It was the forbidden – the private bag. With guilt and a feeling of disloyalty pressing down on me, but with the stronger compulsion to discover what was going on, I opened it. What I found rocked me to the core.

There was a certificate from 1992 detailing the marriage of William and a woman named Michelle; passports for two children – one for a dark-haired baby girl born in 1999 and one for a blond curly-headed toddler boy a few years older; mortgage papers and legal letters to 'Mr and Mrs Jordan'; and birth certificates for two other children unrelated to Michelle, but with Will listed as the father.

It was incomprehensible – like trying to mix oil and water. It did not make any sense and I could not understand the information in front of me at all. I knew Will could lie; in fact, I knew he did it professionally and in some cases automatically, but not to me, not about this kind of stuff! It didn't make sense, didn't fit with the work I knew he did and the person I knew him to be.

The children's passports listed their names as Jordan, but I could not see a resemblance to Will – anyway, that would have been impossible as Will had been infertile, and he was totally astonished to discover we were able to have a child when I conceived Eilidh.

I had to find out what was going on. I texted him to say we had to talk, as something had happened. He came back immediately and

I told him I had found the ring and gone through his bag. It was the ultimate betrayal of his trust and he was irked by it, but he understood why I had done it. He remained calm, as always, and said he once again had to make a call. He would have to tell me everything and needed clearance to do that.

I sat stunned on the couch while he went through to the bedroom to make the call. How could he do that? How could he put the service first? I was so angry that he had put me second again; I needed an explanation, but he would always stick to the rules. He was always the company man. I seethed while I could hear him on the phone.

It took some time and when he came back he looked exhausted. He was in trouble for having left the bag and for getting sloppy. He was angry with himself and upset that I'd had to go through this.

He sat down and looked me straight in the eye, holding my hands.

'Firstly, you are my only wife. I do not have another wife or family,' he started.

The papers all pertained to his asset: a British woman called Michelle who had been recruited in the US by Will into the ODCI after the relationship with her abusive American husband had broken down. Her husband had worked for the Pentagon, so she and her children were already in the system. She was the ideal candidate to bring him back to the UK with her and provide him with a cover story. It was a purely professional relationship through which he got shelter and an identity, whereas she got a regular income and a job, albeit as a silent representative of the US government in the UK.

The marriage certificate was necessary to allow him residency in the country, but was just a forgery created by the ODCI. He was required to carry it and the other papers so that if someone were to stop him – the UK authorities or 'others', as he put it – then everything pointed to the cover and not to his real life.

He had been particularly worried about the incursion into his life by the 'old unsavoury contact' he'd seen in Cambridge and had taken to carrying the papers around with him everywhere so that it would protect us if he was picked up.

Michelle was part of the team – a colleague. Yes, she had children but they were not his and it was purely a working relationship.

He then held my hand tighter and moved a little closer, saying, 'There is something I have to tell you, though . . .'

Then he paused, forcing me to speak for the first time. 'Yes . . . what?'

'I'm not proud of this and I'm worried you will think less of me. I have done things in the past that being with you has made me realise I shouldn't have done.'

'What?' I asked. 'What do you mean?'

'I did have a relationship with Michelle in the beginning. It didn't last long but it was necessary at the start.'

'To recruit her?'

'Yes.' He was ashamed of this and looked down.

I put my hand on top of his, then took it away again. I was still angry but felt distressed at his obvious discomfort. 'What about the mortgage? Why do you have a mortgage and creditor letters in joint names?'

Will went on to tell me that the ODCI had set them up as a couple ten years ago so that he could remain in the country, but that the arrangement was now being dissolved as part of the process of him getting out of the service. Of course they had a mortgage together but it was in name only, and with him being away for so long in the Palestinian territories and unable to get money through to her, the mortgage and bills had not been paid. She had bailiffs at the door and had incurred debts. He told me that he owed her a debt of gratitude because she had stood by him and stayed calm throughout. She'd had to pay debts of his because he had not been there and he owed her money; in fact, she was in a real pickle and might lose the house if he didn't manage to sort the finances out, but the ODCI were being difficult about coming up with the back pay due to his dropping out of active service and moving to a different department.

I felt like my brain, heart and gut were simultaneously being torn in two. There was no one I could talk to about this; no person in whom I could confide except Will, my gentle husband, my confidant and strong friend, my loving partner. I was trapped in silence and had to make a decision for myself. Again, I did not know what to believe. Here was physical evidence of the existence of another wife, but there was an explanation that fitted with the work I knew he did. I had physical evidence of my own marriage to him and also of other things – what was true?

We talked for hours and Will answered every question as best he could, explaining all the details. A lot of the time we went around in circles and he patiently talked it through with me again and again, explaining it from another angle, another perspective, helping me to understand. By the end, I was so weary, and more exhausted than angry or distressed.

'What about the children?' I asked.

'They are Michelle's children,' he said simply. 'You can see that they look absolutely nothing like me.' He spoke to me calmly, caringly, again looking me straight in the eye. 'They are not remotely mixed race.'

'No,' I said, now looking down.

The balance had changed. The guilt had now shifted from him to me. He was only doing his job, living the life he had set up long before he met me so that he could help the brave few defend the world from terror. I had broken his trust and should have known better.

'I trust you,' he said, 'more than I have ever trusted anyone in my life. I understand why you went through the bag. It was my fault, not yours. I shouldn't have left it out, and leaving the ring was stupid. I do not know how that happened.'

'I'm sorry,' I said.

9

Money Drain

July 2004

The holiday over, we drove to London and said goodbye to Will at the airport. He was going to drive back to work at the software company in Cambridge while we flew back to Edinburgh, and would see him the next weekend. I was feeling very confused at this stage and was not wholly convinced by Will's story, but I had little choice other than to believe him. The alternative was just unthinkable.

A couple of days later, the phone rang and Will was on the other end in a complete panic. He was totally frantic; I could hear the fear in his voice. I had never heard him in that kind of state before and it scared me. Had I seen his passport? He had lost it and could not find it anywhere. I went through the bags several times and searched anywhere that it might be. I could not find it. He rang back and asked me to look again: it was 'vital' that it was found. He thought that he must have lost it while at Center Parcs, and I rang them to ask if by any chance they had come across it. The administrator of the park told me that Will himself had been on the phone to them in a blind panic and was desperate to find it, but they did not have it despite a thorough search of the chalet.

I asked Will why he could not just report it as lost, but he explained to me that this was not a real passport. It was a CIA-issue forgery and as such was not something that he could replace now he was no longer on active service. It was something they could use against him and he would have to replace it himself. For some reason, although he had to be rather vague about it, there was no way he could even admit to the authorities that it had gone, and I privately suspected that the ODCI themselves had been into the chalet and stolen it to keep control over him.

Will had to get a new passport from somewhere, and he said that the only way to get out of the hole and out of the service entirely was to buy a new one on the black market. To do this, he needed money. To get out of the service, he also needed a new National Insurance number and he would have to buy that himself as well. He knew the people who could arrange it – the same people who did it for the ODCI – but privately it would cost money. He needed £100,000.

With his salary of £6,000–£10,000 per month it was certainly possible to come up with £100,000 in maybe around a year, but we needed to raise the money now. Time was of the essence and we had to start paying the people who held information over him straight away. At least if we could come up with this sum now, we would be able to repay any loans or capital with his salary. Regarding where the money went, he said that the less I knew about that the better.

The payout from the Jenin massacre had still not materialised, though it was still supposedly in the pipeline, and Will's money from the sale of his house in the US continued to be held up by the American tax authorities. So the credit cards were all maxed out very quickly and Will asked me to organise additional spouse cards, which he used. He was spending money on car rentals – even though he had his own car – and making payments to various companies, including a cinema complex that he part-owned, which he said were simply fronts for contacts of his who were allowing him to move money. Regular payments were less obvious and less traceable than large lumps of cash, and by paying a colleague's satellite subscription he was able to get the cash from the colleague instead. He was taking almost all of his earnings from the business bank account, so I opened a new account to enable him to use the old one for expenses while attempting to maintain some kind of control over the main account. I transferred money that he asked for and started depositing large amounts of cash at his request into an account in the name of M. Hayward. I withdrew between £500 and £2,000 cash at a time from the business account and paid it into Michelle's account – to which he had access and from which he could withdraw funds. Often he sent me to different branches across town to ensure that I was not followed, and if I posted any cash to him I had to ensure that I didn't lick the stamp or envelope and took it into a main post office rather than just putting it into a postbox somewhere.

Then the software-company contract in Cambridge was terminated. Although they were pleased with the work Will was doing, they could not accommodate his erratic behaviour and unexplained absences from work. Although he had another ten days to invoice he had to return the computer equipment first, which he promised daily he would do, but simply never did.

The loss of this income left me with nothing, and the credit cards went over their limits. I remortgaged my flat and raised another £20,000, which I used to reduce the credit-card bills and give Will more cash, but still it was not enough. Every week, there was a new emergency, another need for more money. Each time he promised it would be the last. But each request was more dire, more urgent and with more threats of repercussions for him, then for me and our children.

I decided that it could not continue and asked him for a real picture of what it would take to end this once and for all, to pay them all off and get out. He said that there was only £15,000 still left to pay, but he needed £10,000 immediately. So I made the decision to sell my flat. I borrowed £10,000 from my parents and contacted an estate agent.

◆ ◆ ◆

Within two weeks of putting my lovely flat on the market, it went to closing offers. It was a beautiful property that I had bought in 1990 for £35,000 and had big rooms with a sea view and an original range in the kitchen. I had a lot of wonderful memories of life there and it was my one major asset, but it was more important to protect my family; all I was concerned about was keeping the kids safe. So without looking back, I took the biggest offer of £165,000, which after paying off the original and second mortgage I had already raised for Will left me with £105,000 cash. I paid back my parents and reduced the credit-card bills again, giving Will the additional £15,000 he had requested.

The day I got the cash out of the bank he was being followed, and there was trouble. He had to collect the money in the middle of the night and told me I had to unlock the back door and then stay upstairs with the lights off. We had to be very careful. He was whispering as he came into the room, and it terrified me. He stayed for only a couple of hours, talking frantically and saying that this would make everything all right. But then he had to leave again to ensure that he would not be putting us in more danger – once more leaving me frightened and alone.

But that was not the end of the money drain. Still he needed more and more and more. Eventually it all went. I do not even remember how now. It is almost like looking back at a sharks' feeding frenzy, and I am astonished that I allowed it to happen.

Although I only sold my flat in August 2004, by December 2004 there was nothing left.

10

INCLUDING MY PARENTS

September 2004

During this difficult time, there had been one piece of good news. In July 2004, I had discovered I was pregnant again and we were both happy about it. We had been trying so hard to have another baby and now it was going to happen. I prayed that I was carrying a son and could give Will what he wanted. Maybe it was a sign that things were going to improve, and it certainly seemed to spur Will on to resolve the issues surrounding his work situation and make him more determined to spend time at home.

When we told my family, however, they were not so enthusiastic. My mother was particularly upset because she saw it as putting more pressure on me, and worried about how I would cope.

I depended on my mother so much at this stage. She was always there when Will was not; she was the children's significant other adult and the person I spoke to most days. It was clear by this time that she was deeply suspicious of Will, or at least did not like him any more. She thought he was messing me around and not taking his responsibilities seriously, that he was putting his work before his family, and that he should grow up and start looking after the kids and me. I needed my mother's support and so felt that I had no other choice but to give her an explanation about Will's position. I started to tell her more about Will and about his work. I knew I could trust her to keep my confidences, and as my mother had known people who had worked in British intelligence over the years she could at least understand what I was going through. She was not happy, but being the wonderful person that she was, she did not push the point and stood by me, saying that of course she would be there to help, but warned me to take care and get Will to be home more often.

As our financial problems deepened, however, my parents became more and more unhappy. Through my conversations with my mother, they were aware of what Will did but only in loose terms. Then one day my father tried to approach him about the subject and asked him what the 'other' work entailed and why he had not managed to 'get out' yet. Will was taken aback, as he was not aware that they knew so much, and was very annoyed with me when we got home. He said that he'd had his mobile with him and that the conversation would have been overheard. He said there would be 'consequences' and looked almost frightened. It was unnerving to see him like that.

He was called away almost immediately and told me later that he'd had to face serious physical repercussions. His colleagues had given him a beating, which he could not blame them for: he himself had been involved in similar physical reprisals when others had messed up and given out information. When you understood that the safety and security of the entire team depended on trust and people keeping things under wraps, it was a serious offence to compromise it. I felt awful for being the cause of that. It was not my dad's fault; it was mine for revealing there was more to Will's frequent disappearances than they had thought.

But the good thing that came out of this was that Will now had permission to include my parents in the inner circle of those who knew. I was so grateful for this because it meant that I would have someone I could talk to. I was most keen for my mother to know more in the hope that she would believe Will was loyal to me.

My mother was the closest person to me other than my husband, and she was my dearest friend. She was the only other person that I knew truly loved me, other than Will, and I needed these two people to be on the same side.

When Will came home next, we arranged to visit my parents for the talk. Phones were left behind, coffee made and the four of us sat down. Will told them the whole story from the very beginning: how he had been recruited; how he had worked throughout the world, in Japan, in Brazil and Europe; how he had been in Israel and the Palestinian territories when I was pregnant with Eilidh; and how he was now out of active service and working as a consultant.

He told them at length and in detail about Jenin and the massacre there; how it had upset him and changed his perspective on the service he had dedicated his life to. He wanted out and wanted a normal life. He wanted to provide for me; we would get through this together and he fully appreciated how much support they'd had to give me while he was away, but it would all pay off very, very soon. He reassured them that he loved me. I do not think that my parents fully believed him but, like me, they did not disbelieve him either, and did not see what he planned to gain from saying all this if it was not true. Like me, they gave him the benefit of the doubt. They trusted my judgement and the fact that I believed him. I talked to them about it when Will left again and they seemed more relaxed about our relationship, though it brought up new stresses due to the dangers involved.

Will worked from home when he was there, coding websites privately and working on videotapes and photographs for the MOD and the CIA. He was doing secondment work for the MOD at RAF Brize Norton, specifically verifying video and photographic evidence. He showed me some of the work he was doing and one piece struck me hard. It was a video of the execution of a man called Kenneth Bigley who had been taken hostage in Iraq. Will explained to me how he could tell that the video had been faked because there were inconsistencies in the continuity. Two other American hostages had already been beheaded and Will had verified the videotapes of their executions as real. These had been broadcast on television by now, but I had seen one of them on Will's phone prior to it being aired on the news.

Will told me that Kenneth Bigley had actually been helped to escape by British intelligence, so the video released to the media in early October was suspect. It was eventually reported on the news that Bigley had indeed escaped. However, he was later recaptured by the terrorists and executed anyway. As Will had stated, the first video had not been real – Will said that Kenneth Bigley died from a shot to the head, not beheading. I felt a kind of sickness following the story and didn't question or research it any further.

Will was also verifying photographs of hostages and alleged atrocities perpetrated by American soldiers in Iraq. A lot of the stuff he did appeared on the news a few days later, and the ones he had said were fake were publicly shown to be so. One reason he was doing this work was because of his familiarity with the area: for instance, in one photograph he showed me hostages leaning against a breeze-block wall. Will explained that there were no breeze-block buildings in that region – it was just not a material they used. He then showed me a video of an army vehicle in the Middle East and proved it was fake because you could see its number plate, and they had checked it out; the truck had never left the UK. That video was also exposed on the news as a hoax.

In late October 2004, we were working side by side in our office, he on his computer and me on mine. While writing a report for a business client, I had the BBC newsflash service activated on my PC, and suddenly the news came through that Yasser Arafat had died. As we had a strong connection with the region and Will had spent so much time there, I stopped in astonishment.

'Yasser Arafat is dead,' I said to him, looking over.

He did not look up, stop typing or react in any way; he just said, 'No, he's not.'

'Yes,' I said. 'He is. They just announced it on the news.'

'No, he's not,' Will said simply. 'I would have been told if he had died.'

I raised an eyebrow but just carried on working. I assumed his statement would be explained when he was less focused on what he was doing. Around two hours later, the BBC reported that they had got it wrong. Yasser Arafat was not dead; he was still alive but gravely ill and had been taken to hospital. They had misreported it and Will was right. He did not comment on how he knew, nor would he discuss it; again, it was one of those things that he could not talk about. Yasser Arafat did die relatively soon after that, never coming out of the coma that the media mistook for his death.

Will was not home a lot, but when he was it was certainly interesting. He was still loving, still gentle and it felt good to be part of something bigger than us. He was, after all, working for the good of all.

So life kept going. Although Will was not working on contract now, he was still keeping mobile, travelling all over the country looking for new IT work, as well as keeping one step ahead of the people he was paying to get the documents he needed to extricate himself from the CIA. He kept saying that he had to stay away to protect us and keep the family safe, but would never tell me what he meant by that. He promised weekly, daily, that he would be home, but rarely came. Often he would tell me he was actually on his way and keep in contact while in transit until I thought he was about half an hour away, then he would just disappear for a day, or a few days. I constantly worried for his safety and wondered why he would not tell me if he couldn't get home. I was getting increasingly frustrated with his promises that things were about to change, but still believed him and held on to that hope; after all, our circumstances had improved dramatically before.

Although he had sworn and sworn again that he would be around for this pregnancy, he came home less and less, and again I was living in fear for his life while heavily pregnant and coping with two small children on my own.

11

The Message

October 2004

Then, one day, doubt raised its head again. No, that is not a good way to describe it. One day, something presented itself to me that was incomprehensible and that haunted my sleep for months afterwards.

Will was still away and trying to get work. I was pregnant and working and looking after two small children, panicked and fearful about being discovered by the 'unsavouries' that Will was protecting us from. Then one day Will called me by mistake. I was in a meeting and found he'd left a message on my mobile voicemail service. So without hesitation I sat in the car and listened to it.

It was clear almost immediately that he'd called in error as there were only voices in the background, a woman and children making general conversation. It sounded like a family getting into a car and I was gripped – frozen with the phone to my ear. A woman's voice said, 'Is this yours?' and there were at least two or three children all jabbering, one voice rising up to ask, 'Where are we going, Daddy? . . . Daddy? Where are we going?' Then came Will's voice, uncharacteristically irritated, but definitely his voice.

'Put your seatbelt on, now!' he yelled at the kids, and I went cold through to my bones. I could not believe what I was hearing; it did not make any sense to me at all.

I listened to the message again and again and again. I tried to hear something else, someone else, anything to explain this. I listened to his voice, so irritated, so annoyed. This was not how you spoke to other people's children, but then this was not how I had ever heard him speak to our children, either.

Again, I called him. Again, I said we needed to talk; that I wanted to know what it was all about. The truth! So he came home, carefully checking that he had not been followed.

This time he was not so gentle with his explanation. He was annoyed that I was questioning him again.

'You know about Michelle! You know I have contact with her, and she has children! Why do you put yourself through this?' he said.

I was angry and upset, and I asked him if the children were his. I pointed out that he'd said he'd had a relationship with her in the early days and I needed to know if he'd lied about being infertile. He was hurt and annoyed, saying I should know better than that. He told me that he'd said from the very beginning that he couldn't have kids and it was only his relationship with me that had changed that. Something about our bond, our love, had created life where he'd not been able to before. How could I flout that magic, that miracle, by throwing this in his face?

I asked why one of the children had called him Daddy and he said that he had not been the only man in the car; the boy had been talking to his father, who was loading surveillance equipment into the back of the vehicle and who had answered the boy. Surely I had heard the man answer? 'No,' I said.

I remained unconvinced and kept pushing on. I asked why he had yelled at someone else's kids, then. He answered that he had known them all since they were born and had been the only constant man in their lives; he got irritated with them sometimes and was short with them, particularly if there was any danger of them getting under heavy bits of equipment. He did not remember exactly what had been said, but children loose while equipment was being moved was a bad combination and he had been worried that they would get hurt if they did not sit down.

'They all have different fathers,' he said. None of the real fathers were around much, so Will was the only good male role model for them. He had done his best to provide a stable example for them and looked on them as sort-of family, particularly before he'd had family of his own.

His irritation waned then and again he held my hand, looking with concern into my eyes. 'You know better than this, Mary,' he said. 'You know the situation and I hate that it is so hard on you. I hate that it keeps us apart. Don't you know how hard it is for me, being apart from you and our kids? You are my life and I never knew what living was until I met you.'

Again, we talked for hours until I was simply too tired to think any more. My mother had always said that you should never go to sleep on a fight and I always instinctively try to resolve arguments or strife without sleeping on it. I was exhausted, and Will was still sticking strongly to everything he had said. They were not his kids; they were a family that supported him and gave him a UK base. He answered the same questions over and over, again and again, calmly telling me repeatedly that we were his family and he was telling me the truth.

Again, I gave up and gave him the benefit of the doubt. It fitted with what I knew already, although I never fully believed again. I had a doubt lodged in my mind that grew and struggled to be heard from then on – a seedling of reality trying to survive in the shade of thick, thorny, light-sucking bramble bushes.

12

The Gulf

December 2004

That was the true parting of ways. Life divided into one story or the other. Either he was a loyal, faithful, loving and responsible intelligence agent and husband, or he was a cheating, bigamist liar. It was either/or. I was already far down the path of believing he was my faithful husband and I certainly had no doubt that his job was real, as so much of what he said and did corroborated everything he had told me. His work was who he was, what he lived and breathed. The other fork was already out of reach. I couldn't step across now because there was an unbridgeable ravine between one path and the other.

I could see the other side of that ravine and could see where that path headed – bankruptcy, single motherhood with fatherless children, despair and shame. The path I was on had hope – the constant promise that life was about to improve; the imminent end to the money drain; the promise to resolve the problems and reverse the process; the vows that he would soon be home more; we would be a family and he would provide for the kids. It was the difference between all or nothing – hope or despair.

History was repeating itself. I was alone and pregnant, struggling to survive financially. At least I had my mother to talk to, as she now knew the situation and was supportive rather than critical. She did not like what was going on and was deeply worried about me, but she did her best to hide it because she knew that if she tried to pull me away from Will it would just alienate me. I was trying to be so strong and show her I was coping, but at least I could talk to her about some of the stuff I was going through. I shared my feelings of being lonely or frightened, angry or sad, and she was always there for me.

The other members of my family were equally concerned and my sister tried to get Will to come back several times, writing him emails with the aim of sparking his sense of responsibility. On one occasion, just before the birth of our second child, she wrote:

> *Dear Will,*
>
> *I am writing to you to ask what you are up to? My little sister, Mary, is about to give birth to your second child and is getting quite tired and could do with the support. Do you think it is about time that you came home to look after her and your family? Mary will be able to deal with anything and talk through any problems about work, money issues or whatever if that is what is keeping you away.*
>
> *Please be honest with Mary – it is the lynchpin of any good relationship. Family life is time-consuming, hard work, frustrating and sometimes, hopefully, very satisfying and fun (as you probably already know). If that is getting to you, then let Mary know.*
>
> *I find my children drive me nuts from time to time and it makes all the difference having [my partner] here at the end of the day to talk to. I don't*

honestly know how Mary is coping on her own while
you're not around.

> *Mary doesn't tell me any details of what you are*
up to but I had to write and tell you my concerns and
stick up for my sister and my nieces.
> *Your concerned sister-in-law, Mary's sister,*
Isobel

Will would reply telling Isobel how much he loved the kids and me, and how much he wanted to be with us if he possibly could.

For a while she would feel better and feel that he was making an effort, but, as with me, the feeling would fade when he did not appear.

This particular time, Will started to open up a little more to Isobel, explaining that he and I had not fallen out at all and there was nothing on this earth that he would rather do than be home taking care of our children, both the two that were already here and our unborn baby. If anything, the tension between us was the product of unfulfilled love, a result of our frustration at not being able to support each other as we would choose to do in other circumstances.

He envied the closeness we had in our family and it hurt him that she thought he didn't care about the welfare of his wife and children. There was so much more he would have liked to say to her and he wished that he could explain the situation more clearly. But he assured her that time would heal all things and history, particularly with 'its fuller disclosure of all the surrounding circumstances', would be a kinder judge of his actions. That, he said, would be his only comfort as he continued to do what he could to get back home to me and the children.

He went on to say that nothing short of 'life and death' would prevent him from being by my side for the birth of our child: 'I have not left Mary . . . she is my wife, now and for the rest of my life and I intend to spend the rest of my life with her and with our family. No matter what happens, nothing changes that . . . I am only half of all that I could ever be without her . . .'

He agreed with Isobel, assuring her that he knew I was all that she could ever describe me to be and so much more, just as only her partner could truly know Isobel and all that she was, and all that she brought to him. He said that he was proud to be able to call her his sister-in-law.

◆   ◆   ◆

In his absence, we were getting deeper and deeper into debt. The credit cards were at their limit but Will continued to use them on a daily basis. Eventually the credit-card companies put a stop on my accounts, but not until the cards were all 50 per cent over their limits, one with a balance of £15,000. Even then, Will continued to use the cards for small amounts, £20 or £30 here or there, several times a day. These would slip through the system and be allowed by the companies taking the payments from him.

Each time more charges appeared on the cards, Will promised that it was the end of it – the last he would need. Often he would say that there had been a mistake, so I called the credit-card companies and disputed several payments that he denied, even getting replacement credit cards as he thought the ODCI colleagues were messing around to make a point.

Towards the end of December 2004, however, the situation was getting more and more desperate. I had no money left from the sale of my house and no credit left. All my money was gone, but Will still needed more. One day, he called me in a complete panic.

'Something has come up; it's my fault, as it's something I over-looked . . . someone . . . I overlooked. This is as serious as it gets. I need two thousand pounds today. It has to be today! Can you think of anything, Mary?'

'No,' I said, defeated.

'What about your brother or your sister? Can they lend it to us? I'll be able to repay it within a couple of weeks. This is really serious, Mary! Just don't tell them what it's for! It's better if they just think it's for you.'

He told me that it would all have been for nothing if I did not manage to get the money; that we would lose everything and that the physical danger was very, very real.

I was desperate. Will had already taken everything I had, but if I didn't raise this £2,000 then all would be lost. I asked my brother if he would lend me the money. Will had suggested heavily that I shouldn't tell him what it was for, but I wasn't about to start lying now – it was against my principles. In the end I told him that I needed it for Will but couldn't explain why, and my brother came to my rescue.

He came to the house with £2,000 in cash for me and asked if everything was all right. I was still trapped, though. Everything was so far from all right that I was not even sure if anyone would believe me, and if I talked about my suppressed suspicions it might make them real and true. I believed I was in physical danger, that I was being watched and there was a possibility of being overheard – if I told my brother what was going on I would be putting him in danger too.

So I said that everything was fine and would be OK. I smiled and asked him how he was, as he had problems of his own. I thanked him gratefully and as soon as he left I phoned Will to tell him I had the money he needed. He came home briefly to pick up the cash, then said he had to go out for a few hours to put it where it was needed before doing some Christmas shopping. Although he didn't have much cash, he really wanted to get something for the children and me, which at the time I thought was touching. He was pleased with me because at the very least the cash would allow him to be home with us for Christmas; however, he didn't appear and I didn't see him again until briefly in January 2005.

At that point, he stayed for a few days but soon vanished again, and I was really feeling the strain on our relationship. He promised to be home almost daily, saying that he was in the car and actually driving up. On numerous occasions, he asked me to scrape together £100 for petrol money, and I would empty every account to get it, only for him not to show up. Sometimes he told me he had run out of money and had to sleep in the car without food; mostly he ran out of phone credit and was unable even to call me, and switched his phone off so that he could sleep. Sometimes he suspected that he was being followed and so would turn around instantly without calling because he did not want to lead any 'unsavouries' home to us.

I confided in my mum that I was getting pretty annoyed at his disappearing, but could not tell her about the physical threats he was protecting us from because it would worry her too much.

I was getting more and more suspicious, as Will's promises were not fulfilled and he still had not found work that would support the family. Then in January 2005, our mobile phones were barred for outgoing calls as I had not paid the contract bill, and I had to pick up voicemail from a landline. As both his phone and mine were on a contract under my name, I suddenly discovered that I could pick up his voicemail this way, too. If I only picked up the first message and did not save or delete it, then he would not know I had done it; and if he could not tell, then no one else could, either.

I became addicted to picking up his messages. I craved proof one way or the other – something to tell me what was going on.

Through tapping into his voicemail this way I found out that Michelle was angry with him because he'd taken her car and vanished with it – he had said he was going to the chemist's and just not returned; I found out he was buying a house – he later told me that he was just going through the motions of this for the sake of appearances; I found out that their nanny had not been paid and the agency was displeased, very displeased at being messed around; I found out that he was indeed continuing his cover story with Michelle. It didn't sound to me as if there was any warmth or love between them. Her tone sounded very businesslike, as she left messages in which she seemed to bark at him and state the facts of what needed to be done.

I still had no proof.

In February 2005, Will contacted me again, desperately in need of £5,000. By then, however, I had nothing left and could not borrow any more from the banks or credit cards. I asked my brother again for help, without any real desire for him to say yes, and he asked if it was for me or for Will. When I told him that it was for Will, he said, 'No, then.' I genuinely blessed my brother for that even at the time, because I had realised by this point that Will's need for money was a bottomless pit. But still I could not give up hope and, like a gambler who has already lost everything but finds one more pound in his pocket, I searched for any last source from which I could squeeze some cash. In the end, I sold my life-insurance policy – the only thing I had left, the endowment I had taken out for the flat – and raised the last £5,000 for my husband, because what else could I do?

Our rent was not being paid and the landlords started to hassle me. Will promised that he had paid it into their account and it was all getting sorted. This line was starting to wear thin and I had heard it all before.

By March 2005 I was eight months pregnant and had no money to pay for food, let alone rent or bills. I had nothing. I swallowed any remaining pride I had left and asked my mother if we could come and stay with them before the baby was born. My parents took us in without judgement and with all good grace. They fed us and provided me and the girls with company and support – with the baby soon coming it was a lifeline that gave me a small sense of being grounded again.

Will still insisted that the rent on the house had been paid and said he was talking directly with the landlords to sort out why they'd not received it, and I just left him to it. Contact with Will seemed to be drifting away. I had not seen him since January and I was getting fewer and fewer emails and texts, even though each text or email promised he was on his way home at the time.

Then, two weeks before I gave birth to our son, I received a desperate email from Will. It was another request for a large amount of cash, just like so many before it, but this time it went into far more detail and explained why we were being put through so much.

It was 16 March 2005 and Will opened by saying that this was probably the most difficult email he had ever had to write to me. He was about to divulge confidential information but he felt he had no choice, as my safety and that of our family was at stake. He could only hope that I would understand and perhaps even forgive him for some of the decisions he had made that had led us to this point.

Will then warned me that he would not be able to state things plainly but would talk slightly in code. He said that I already knew some of what he had been involved with in the past, and it was best not to put too much information in any one email. It was safe for him to say, however, that in the course of some of the domestic business he'd had to engage in he had been involved with many 'less-than-savoury' characters and even organisations who were sources for information, light arms, even personnel at times. In particular, his last domestic assignment, which required heavy immersion in the British Muslim community, involved several dangerous people. He said that this was 'typically done via an intermediary', someone who was already involved and trusted but who had become disaffected. During his last assignment, that intermediary, whom he named, was the son of a 'Bradford-based businessman who had connections with anti-Western activities across the North region for many years'.

Will had talked to me at length about this sort of thing in the past, but had never put it in writing. Now he was telling me in detail about an intelligence assignment where he'd had to recruit someone to get him into a group that they needed information on. He was telling me the details and the people involved. It shook me to the core because it was unprecedented and heralded some major problems if he felt the need to tell me about it. It meant either he was in immediate physical danger, or that we were. I was terrified and fascinated all at the same time.

According to Will, his contact's younger brother had been killed during the 2001 summer riots and it was this loss that caused him to question his involvement in his father's operations, and whether they were really in line with the teachings of his faith. Will used these doubts to befriend him and persuade the young man to help him infiltrate the community.

Once the assignment was completed, Will extricated himself, following the normal procedures, and as far as he was concerned that was the end of the matter. He had not, however, banked on running into the same young man after taking on the contract for the software company in Cambridge. During his second month there, he was introduced to a database analyst intern 'visiting' from Pakistan. This was his young contact, who had changed his appearance and assumed a different identity. The problem was that he also recognised Will.

Will described how he had been discovered by a 'mark', and that this was why his job in Cambridge had fallen away. This was why our lives had suddenly become so fraught. I was starting to see where the story was going, but still did not understand why Will was telling me all this now, and in such a detailed way.

He went on to explain that with my financial help he had been able to construct an exit ID for leaving the CIA. He had to make sure that all of his traces from the software company in Cambridge would point to the Oxford base – i.e. Michelle – instead of to Scotland and his real family. But Will believed that the contact had informed other operatives of his whereabouts – particularly as someone had looked up his registration number at the company he was working for. What followed was the madness of contacting anybody else who might be implicated and helping them to leave immediately in order to avoid serious repercussions.

Will explained that his activities since leaving the company in Cambridge had been about trying to 'get lost' and sever all ties with anyone that could point in the wrong direction – specifically to us. There had been a lot involved with that, and it had become more difficult when he lost access to some of the privileges of his real employer, the CIA. He'd had to enlist the aid of some of those 'less-than-desirables' and 'do some less-than-desirable things', for which he was sorry. 'It was only because I truly was afraid for your safety, and theirs as well, and with the baby on the way, I just could not take the risk of leaving anything undone.'

This sent a shiver down my spine and I started racing through the rest of the message. If Will was afraid for our safety, then we were in serious danger. He had always had supreme confidence in his ability to protect us and keep us safe. He seemed less sure now and that got my full attention. For once, this did not seem to be about money, but then it became clear what he needed and why he had gone into so much detail. He wrote:

> Mary, I need you to do something for me. I know it will go against everything you have said and it will be a source of great grief for you, possibly even costing you your relationship

100

with others in your family for a time. I need
you to know that it is the only reason that I
am telling you all of this and that it is only in
utter desperation that I am writing this. I need
to, without being able to make any promise of
repayment time, borrow £5,000.

He needed £3,000 by Friday and £2,000 within the next week.
If I could confirm to him that this would be possible then he could
'give instructions to someone to do what was necessary now' and
then be home to stay by Thursday.

My spirits sank; I knew that there was no way I could raise that
kind of money.

Will went on to explain that his plan for the future was to
find whatever work was available, ideally in Edinburgh or the
surrounding area, then to start over financially and personally,
building back up what had been lost. He would have to keep the
creditors at bay, with promises and guile, then work as hard as
possible to pay them off. He desperately wanted to enjoy the first
months of our son's life and rediscover his daughters once again,
not to mention his wife. He said that he could not do this any
other way. There was no alternative and he was unable to tell me
what would happen if I could not help him. He said that in the
past he had always tried to play down the risks involved in what
he did, but this was no longer possible. As he pointed out, he had
'never cried wolf before'.

Most importantly, Will went on to say that under no circumstances was I to confide in anyone about what was going on. It was
not something that anyone else could ever be aware of, no matter
how difficult that might be for me. He emphasised that I could not
discuss the situation with my family: 'They must never know about
this, Mary, for all our sakes.' He realised that this might mean I had

to lie in order to get hold of the money. He was guilt-ridden about the situation but there was no other way. The only concession he would make was that, after it was all over, if I wanted to know what his 'instructions' had been, he would tell me, though of course I would not be able to tell anyone else. He also promised that he was not putting anyone's life at risk.

Will said he had spent hours trying to work up the courage to send the message but there was nothing else for it now. He said he truly had no choice, and was saddened that the first proper contact he had been able to have with me in two months was something like this, and something to worry me with before the birth of our son.

But despite all the veiled threats the message contained, there was nothing that I could do; and although he promised to come home if I could sort it out, I did not believe he would. I knew I had nothing else to sell or any means to raise more money, and I would not lie to my family. This was our mess, not theirs, and I would not get them into the same debt and situation that I was trapped in, particularly not by deception. A line had been drawn in my head and in my heart. It stopped here. Enough. I was broken and had failed my husband and the father of my children; I had nothing left and nothing left to give.

I cried in defeat and acceptance that it was all gone, and then wrote back to Will.

Oh my love,

I really don't know what I can do . . . it is not a matter that I can borrow any more money from any members of my family . . . they will not lend it to me. Neil and Isobel have both spent the money that they had available. I don't think that they would lend me even if I begged because I have not paid Neil back the £2,000 borrowed on Xmas Eve. Will, I really really really do not know where I could get that money from. I am totally broke and have tried to raise credit for myself just to survive!

I don't know what I can do, I really don't. £5,000 is just totally beyond anything that I could raise now. I have nothing else to sell and how could I even go about asking for it from anyone?

God Will, you surely know that don't you, what could I possibly do?

Will replied that evening, asking again for me to think of something. He said: 'I can only say that if there is any way that even in your wildest imagination you can envisage, this is the time for it . . . this is the moment for the long shot.'

He was begging for my help and clearly struggling with it. He acknowledged that he was a poor excuse for a husband right now, and said again how sorry he was.

I felt desperate, but there was nothing I could do. Nothing. I knew I had let him down and that it was probably all over, but in a way I also knew that otherwise it would never be over; part of me was relieved that I had nothing left to give.

13

STARTING TO PREPARE

April 2005

After Will's second begging email, I repeated that there was nothing I could do. I didn't hear back from him and was scared for his life. I spent the days afterwards texting and emailing him, wanting confirmation that he was still there and still alive. He would answer but only with fleeting comments, and said that he had to be on the move most of the time. He said he understood that I was unable to help him and forgave me. Under no circumstances would he tell me anything about what he was doing, except that he would sort it out so that he could be home for the birth of our son. I was to text him when I went into labour, and he would be there, come hell or high water.

Our son was born on 1 April 2005. I texted Will when my contractions started and he said that he was on his way and would definitely be there. Once again, my mother took me to the hospital and was by my side, holding my hand. This time, the birth was more straightforward, with the contractions doing all the pushing, leaving me feeling rather on the periphery. At least I had gas and air to help with the pain rather than just oxygen!

By now, I was so good at controlling my outward expressions that the midwives had no idea how close to delivery I actually was. I calmly told them that the baby was coming, but because I was not screaming they did not take me that seriously. The midwife commented on how relaxed I was about the process just as my waters exploded with the most amazingly powerful contraction, taking her by surprise. As she was at the receiving end, she was soaked from her chest to her shoes. Then, without giving us time to react and without any pushing by me at all, Zach shot out into the world like a rugby ball. He was a beautiful 9 lb 10 oz bouncing baby boy with an expression of complete surprise at his rude entrance into the world.

As my mother had to get back to relieve my dad of looking after my two daughters, she had not expected to stay long enough to see my son born. But Zach appeared no more than twenty minutes after we arrived at the hospital, so she hadn't had time to leave. I was glad she was there and glad I'd had someone to share the experience with. My mother was impressed, having seen me give birth twice, with no more than gas and air on one occasion to help with the pain, and I never yelled or screamed. I had managed to focus on the outcome rather than the pain, and enjoyed the experiences rather than being afraid of them. It was indicative of my overall approach to life.

Zach was perfect and, after instantly falling in love with him, I spent hours gazing at him in amazement. Once again, however, throughout the twelve hours I was in hospital I was constantly awaiting the arrival of my husband, frequently glancing at the door. When I telephoned him and asked where he was, I was told he was still on his way but would be there imminently. He did not appear while I was in hospital and, although he sent me texts saying how proud he was of me and our son, he did not appear after I got home either.

My family were getting seriously worried about me now, and were very concerned that Will had failed to show up for the birth of his child a second time. My sister Isobel wrote again to Will expressing her concern about me and trying to help in the only way she could think of; but, like me, she only got promises that he would be there if he could.

My image of being pregnant and having a baby was of being pampered and looked after for nine months. I would be brought ice cream and pickles for a craving in the middle of the night and then, when the baby was born, my husband and I would nudge each other to say 'your turn' to get him. I had pictured it as a mutual experience shared between two grown-ups who loved each other. The reality was somewhat different. I'd had three babies, all pretty much alone. I knew that Zach was my last baby and I would never do this again, so I gave up on that dream.

Will met his son in May 2005 after I finally talked directly to the landlords of the rented house and voluntarily agreed to move our stuff out and into storage. Will had been travelling all over the country trying to sort out the mess he was in because I had not managed to raise the money he needed. He had been sleeping in his car and was living a very uncomfortable existence. As always, though, he would not discuss the details or tell me what was going on, saying it was better I did not know. To get any future work at all, Will needed the servers, so he came to pick them up when I moved out, as well as the taser, which I did not want to take to my parents' home.

Zach was, by then, six weeks old, and Will was totally bowled over by him. He held his son in his arms and played with him, and it gave me such a wonderful feeling of joy to see them together. I was hurt and upset at Will for not coming back for the birth, and gutted that I had gone through the experience without him again, but that was in the past and I have never been one to hold on to grievances. Will swore to me that even coming back for the servers was risky, so once again I let it all go. We spent a couple of days packing up the house and putting everything we had into storage, then Will drove off with the servers in the car.

In June 2005, things suddenly improved. Will had found another contractor who could work for the company. Her name was Alice and he'd secured a contract for her to work in procurement – with our company acting like a temp agency, she would do the work and we would bill the contractor, then give her a weekly payment for a set hourly rate. I did not see the contract, as he signed it himself, but she was apparently going to earn the company £415 per day. It therefore seemed suspicious to me that she had agreed to work for £800 per week in return, and I queried this with Will on several occasions. Will was adamant that it was all OK, saying that she was getting much more than she had been paid before, and once she'd been with us for a few months he'd promised to give her a pay rise or take her on as an employee. We'd see how it went for the first three months.

I wanted to speak to Alice, so Will gave me her number but said that she was rather nervous. He told me that he'd known her as an administrator working for the CIA in the UK many years ago and had bumped into her again recently. She'd been in an abusive relationship and was recovering from that. He suggested that I should not mention that we were married, as that might diminish her confidence in the company. I spoke to her and got her bank account details so that I could deposit her money, and asked her to confirm the £800 per week payment, which she did.

Will told me that she was to get money weekly for the first four weeks, then monthly, so I arranged that with the bank, and Alice started working in July 2005.

Then Will got himself a contract working for the Office of the Deputy Prime Minister (ODPM) in central London. With all the terrorist activities going on and particularly the July London bombings I was seriously unhappy about this, but he was keen to take the job. He seemed to take my concerns seriously but the need to work was greater, and he saw this as a good opportunity. He would be working as an IT contractor on a new finance system for the office and it could really lead him places.

I wondered how he had managed to land this role, as they do security checks on new employees, but he said that it was easy to get through. The agency who had offered him the contract had asked him to bring along identification on his first day, specifically his passport, which he no longer had. He told me how he'd found ways around their security, simply by confidently stating that the checks had already been done and his passport copied the week before. Whatever he did, it was successful, and he started work in August 2005. From a purely civilian point of view, I found the ease with which he'd bypassed our government's internal security disturbing.

So the company now had two income streams and money started to come in again. It was paid into the business accounts and Will would agree with me what money I could take to start paying off the debts he had accrued. Then he would take the rest, asking me to deposit it into the old business account which he used for 'expenses', and into the M. Hayward account which he had access to. There was not enough left for VAT or tax, but Will kept saying that VAT didn't threaten physical violence and could wait.

What could not be ignored, however, were the frequent demands from the finance company through which we had purchased the Mercedes 4x4. The payments had fallen behind by several months and they wanted me to bring the account up to date, but there was no way that I could. Again and again I asked Will to take the car back, at least. I even threatened him with calling the police but I really don't know what I would have said to them if I had. Every day he promised its imminent return. Then it developed a fault and went into a Mercedes garage in England for repairs, so he physically couldn't get it back home. The finance company got fed up with his excuses and took me to court.

Will talked to the finance company's lawyers direct and arranged for payment terms before the actual court date, so that the appearance would be a formality. The terms he'd arranged were £950 per month, which was totally unrealistic. He would not listen to me when I said we could not manage to pay that, and just told me to trust him.

Going to court was another extremely uncomfortable experience. I was completely unfamiliar with the process and it terrified me. I couldn't believe how much my life had changed over the past five years. Before I met Will, I had rarely even received a red bill, and although I had not been brilliant with money I had £2,000 in savings, a flat that I had been paying a mortgage on for ten years, a life-insurance policy and a good solid job. Now I was standing in a courtroom for non-payment of debts. I used to feel that the world was my oyster; I was happy-go-lucky, cheerful and fun. Now I was frightened all the time, I couldn't sleep and felt trapped in my own life. The worst of it all was that although I could see how I had changed, I could not see a way back to the person I had been before.

Up to that point, I had tried to look upon new experiences as expanding my horizons. For instance, I used to be scared of heights, so I did a bungee jump to face the fear and not have it control me. I tried hard to put going to court into that category, but it was extremely unpleasant. I sat in the car and cried for an hour before the hearing. I was so far out of my depth that I felt I was drowning by degrees. Will had sworn that he would not let me go to court alone, that he would be there, but by now I did not even raise an eyebrow at his failure to appear. I was used to being left high and dry. I had expected it, in fact.

The court itself was actually quite a straightforward place and nothing really to fear. In my mind I had envisaged it being like the courtrooms you see on television, with wooden panelling and a raised dock in which I would have to stand. In reality, it was quite different. The room had five rows of seats laid out theatre-style on either side of the central door. In the middle was a long table running at a right angle to the judge's raised desk, allowing the two opposing sides to face the judge in front.

When I walked in there were various people sitting waiting for their hearing, vastly outnumbered by the legal staff in robes and wigs who were there to represent their clients both present and absent. I asked a young female lawyer what I should do, and she told me to check the list on the desk to see when my case was scheduled, then sit and wait to be called, which I did.

It is hard and belittling to stand up in front of a stranger who is looking down on you, literally, and passing a legal judgement. The whole process is beyond your control and leaves you feeling degraded. When my name was called, I felt as if my limbs were suddenly impossibly heavy; it was like wading through cold porridge as I walked to the front of the room. I could feel the scrutiny of the other ten or so uncomfortable people who were awaiting their own hearings.

The lawyer for the finance company spoke to confirm that there was an agreement in place. The judge bawled him out because they had messed up the legal document, stating that they wanted the total value of the car in cash 'plus' the car itself, rather than 'or', which was asking a little much! Also, they had not mentioned legal costs. Then he turned to me and asked a few questions, though what they actually were, I don't remember. Then I was told it was over. I had no idea what had happened or what had been decided. I had been there only in body, but apparently Will's offer had been accepted and the first payment was to be made at the end of the month. I just could not believe that this would actually happen.

Needless to say, the payments were not made and within a month the court ordered the return of the car – but I didn't have it.

The whole point of the charade in court was to buy Will another month's use of the car. I had gone through that discomfort just so he could postpone the inevitable. I wrote to the lawyers saying that it was in a Mercedes garage in England and I have not heard a word from them since.

In the meantime, my maternity leave over, I started working as a marketing consultant and motivational trainer again and decided to look for a flat to move into. I was still living with my parents at this point and I needed to find a place of my own, where I could find my own feet and survive independently of Will. He had told me that he was at last starting to turn things around, but I couldn't depend on just that. So in August 2005, I found a wonderful place where the rent was not too expensive and moved myself and the three kids in.

Will was around occasionally, sometimes every other weekend. Not long after my move, we even managed a trip to London while my sister Isobel looked after the children – a couple of days away in a hotel. We finally went to *Phantom of the Opera* and then to a Japanese restaurant where the staff seemed to recognise Will, greeting him warmly. When I queried how they knew him, Will explained that he ate lunch there often. The restaurant was a lovely place where the customers sat around three sides of the cooking plate itself and the chef cooked the food right in front of you. The chef bantered with Will and we both enjoyed his performance. The food was delicious and the evening was fun.

He frequently spoke on the phone to Alice while we were away, and explained to me that she was being harassed by her abusive ex and needed someone to talk to. She had become pretty disillusioned during her time with the CIA, he continued – not unreasonably, as they had misused her. So when she vanished one day a couple of months after our trip to London, it did not seem too odd. Will was seriously annoyed about it but said that her uncle had died and she'd gone to support her mother through her grief.

He brought home the servers from wherever they had been. But as there was no room to set them up in my flat, and no desire on my part, he only connected up the small email server in the cupboard, and we put the other hard drives and servers into storage.

In October 2005, my brother Neil and his fiancée Cathy asked us over to dinner one evening, and it was one of the rare occasions when Will actually managed to turn up. Neil is a forty-six-year-old rugby player with the right physique for his sport and can drink anyone I know under the table. He is a good-time boy and enjoys life to the full, having no children to tie him down and having found the perfect woman to share the fun with. Neil had decided it was about time he got to know my husband better, and also decided to test him to the limit. Will could not hold his alcohol at all. If he had a couple of drinks, he started to talk and say things he shouldn't, and I had often found out more than he would usually let on by topping up his glass.

I was nervous that Will would compromise himself by talking to my brother if he got too drunk, so we agreed on a code word, 'Uncle', that I would say if Will was revealing too much and would regret it in the morning.

It was a very pleasant and relaxed evening. We had a lovely meal and the four of us were getting on extremely well. My brother's flat is very comfortable and we sat in the lounge after dinner with the boys drinking more wine as Will talked with increasing openness about his work. Halfway through the evening, I gave up saying the code word and openly stated to Will that he should probably not continue with the conversation. My brother had plied him with enough alcohol to sink a largish boat, and there were at least six empty red-wine bottles sitting around. Considering that I was not drinking as I was driving and Cathy had only had a couple of glasses, you can imagine the state the boys were in.

Even my brother does not remember everything that was said, but he does recall Will demonstrating his ability to speak Hebrew, Spanish and Japanese, and relating the atrocities that occurred in

Jenin during the massacre. Will explained how he had survived in the rubble and how he and his team had had to evade the regular troops until they could be picked up by their own people. He talked about his missions and assignments abroad; about things he had been asked to do for the CIA; about how he had got into the service in the first place and how he had lost faith in what he was doing now. He even talked about the assassination of John F. Kennedy and said that it was a specialist CIA-issue Teflon-coated bullet that had been used. It was impossible for a civilian to have possession of such a bullet at the time, meaning that the CIA did have a hand in the killing.

Will rolled and reeled, drunk beyond measure, before heading for the bathroom. When he didn't return, we went to check on him. He was hunched over the toilet, a sickly green colour and was vomiting repeatedly. He stayed in the bathroom all night and we even moved a mattress in there for him as he vomited again and again into the toilet. Cathy is a nurse and checked on him at regular intervals, worried that he had alcohol poisoning, so I left him there to recover, going back to the children and our babysitter.

After that night, Neil was finally convinced that Will was who he said he was. My husband had passed my brother's impromptu test, and another member of my family knew and understood what I had been living alone with for five years. Although I was worried that Will would regret it, the night made me feel more secure. Now that Will himself had told someone else what was going on, I would get the support and understanding I needed without breaking the code of silence.

Will was ill for a couple of days but said he had enjoyed the evening and did not regret what he had said. He added that he trusted my brother and his fiancée, and if it helped me to cope, then all the better.

14

GET-OUT-OF-JAIL-FREE CARD

November 2005

In November 2005, Will was arrested. He rang to ask me to call the Office of the Deputy Prime Minister and say he had been delayed getting to work. Everything was fine, he said. It had been a misunderstanding with the Mercedes garage, who had charged the wrong credit card for the work they'd done; the situation would be easily resolved. He would be able to get out quickly because he had a word he could use that highlighted he was part of the intelligence community.

He was blasé about it and quite calm, so I did as he asked and told the ODPM that he had been delayed. His boss was fine about it and told me not to worry.

Later that day, I received a phone call from the police about the Mercedes. They asked me where the car was, as it was in my name. I told them my husband was driving it in England. They thanked me and hung up. Will was furious with me for telling them that. He said I had put us all at risk, but I could not see how. He said that the police were not all they seemed and were part of a bigger picture. I asked how someone knowing he was driving the car put us at risk. He told me that they now knew I was his wife and therefore could use the kids and me as a way to get to him. I could not understand why it mattered so much to Will, but then I also did not realise at the time what a dramatically pivotal moment this was to be for him.

Will sighed and reassured me that everything would be OK, he would sort it out, but added that things would get worse before they got better.

'It's going to be a bumpy ride,' he said, 'and now is the time to decide what you truly believe.'

If nothing else, I knew that the job was real – the CIA, the danger and the fear. I chose to believe in him and trusted him to keep us all safe.

During the ongoing investigation into his activities, the Office of the Deputy Prime Minister was informed of his arrest for fraud and terminated his contract. So once again he had no income. Again, I was on my own financially and also supporting his insatiable requests for cash.

15

The Last Visit

January 2006

Will had promised faithfully that he would be back for Christmas but, as usual, something more pressing came up. He told me that he was protecting us and it was more important that he kept the family safe, particularly now. I did not complain about his absence, though I did complain about the business account being used to pay for another hire car. The account that he was using had been put into overdraft by a £750 payment for a hire car I knew nothing about. He said it was a mistake and would sort it out.

When he came back in early January, we celebrated Christmas together with the kids and opened presents – the many we had for him and the ones he had brought for us. Our family enjoyed being whole for the last time. He played with his kids and cuddled his wife. He helped clean up and made dinner. He told me that he was home now, that things had changed; he would find work, normal work, very soon, because at last he was out of the service.

There was still trouble ahead, though – still the fallout to face. The police had found the taser in the car when they had arrested him, as well as papers that pertained to his cover story. As some of them related to his asset Michelle, the police were talking about charging him with bigamy. It would all be OK, though, because the documents were fakes and the police would have to find an actual marriage registration to make the charge stick. This, of course, did not exist, because he was not really married to Michelle. The official Department of Central Intelligence would make it all go away, and even if they did not, the charges of bigamy, fraud and possession of firearms would get him only a couple of months in jail. He could easily handle that. In fact, he thought it would be a bit of a holiday for him, not having to run and hide all the time. He kept saying that he was relieved, because without this hanging over him he would be free. They could not charge him twice for the same crime and he would be home for good once he got out.

Given his cheerfulness about the whole situation – he was almost buoyant – I felt reassured. I am a positive thinker and hoped for the best. I did not want him to go to jail – the idea terrified me – but he seemed at ease with the prospect. As a black belt in karate, he did not fear anyone inside and already knew what to expect.

He had only been home for a couple of days when he got a call from a company asking him to come in for an interview the next day. Again there seemed to be hope that he could pull it all back together at last.

That night, we spent time talking and being together. I took a shower and he joined me. We washed each other and stood naked in each other's embrace. Afterwards we sat on the bed and he dried my long hair. My hair had been short when I met him and I had only grown it long because he'd expressed a preference for it that way. He sat behind me and stroked it, expertly using the combination of drier and brush to make it a wonderful, affectionate experience.

It was somehow more intimate than making love – more of an expression of emotion than anything I had known before. When my hair was dry, I lay back on the bed and we kissed. He told me that he loved me and I made his life worth living, that until we'd met he hadn't known what love was, or what family meant. Then he told me again with his body, kissing me all over and using his hands to arouse further heights of passion in me. It was the ultimate expression of love: pure, untainted, unrestrained. It was gentle and exciting, indescribably profound. I loved him then more than ever before, with every part of me. I knew he loved me and had no doubt about his loyalty or devotion.

In the morning, he left for his interview and said he would be back that evening. It was the last time I ever saw my husband.

Will didn't make it home that night and although he daily texted, rang and emailed saying he was on his way, he never came back. Each time he failed to show up he said he could not say why, and I knew better than to ask because it just caused tension between us. I guessed that he was once again ducking and diving, keeping the 'undesirables' away from home and sleeping in his car.

He told me that the interview had been successful and the company were interested in taking him on. They wanted a reference, though, and Will had given my name as the person to call. He needed this job to get back on track and he needed my help to do it.

I was desperately nervous about the impending telephone call and was stumped as to what I would say.

'What if they ask me technical questions? What if they want to know details?' I said.

Will told me they just wanted to know that he was reliable and would do a good job. Well, I knew he would do a good job if left alone by the service to get on with it. Reliable? If the service did not drag him away again, then he could be. I agreed to do it.

Will coached me and once again I was put in a position where I had to lie for him. Having spent a few years as a theatre actress, I can pull a confident voice out of the hat if required, but inside

I was shaking. His potential new boss, a chap called Christopher, rang and we talked. He asked questions and I answered them, telling him that Will was good at his work, which as far as I knew was true. He asked about his reliability and I said it was fine. He asked what his biggest weakness was and I laughed. 'Timekeeping,' I said. The truth just popped into my head. I told him that there had been an occasion when Will's timekeeping problems had eventually lost him the contract; however, it was a particularly stressful time in his life and I would be surprised if it happened again. I felt awful lying to this man. I think that deep down I was trying to warn him, and that the lies had got to me.

Christopher thanked me and offered Will the post.

16

THE CHARGES

A couple of weeks later, I got a phone call from Will, sounding serious. His tone made me instinctively know I had to sit down.

'We have to talk,' he said. 'Something has happened that you need to know about.'

I went cold.

He continued. 'You know about the investigation. Well, the police are going to charge me.' He told me that they were going to charge him with bigamy and firearms offences – they had taken his possession of my CIA-issue taser more seriously than he'd expected. I instantly felt guilty because he was being punished for trying to help me feel safer – which was why he had got the taser in the first place. They were also going ahead with the charge of fraud, which was just a misunderstanding, he assured me, and would be cleared up relatively easily.

'But there is something else, too,' he said. 'Ten years ago, I had to do an assignment during which I had to get information out of a particularly nasty person who was in a sex offenders' prison. To get close to him, I had to go inside, and a charge was raised to allow me to do this.'

'What?' I asked.

The service had set up a scenario using a teenage girl, who would make the allegation. He told me he was handed a fifteen-month pass into jail but got the information from his contact within seven months, and was out as soon as he succeeded in his assignment. The service removed the files but they had been revived as they were trying to make an example out of him. Because the file was live again, he was being charged with not registering his address under the Sexual Offences Act, something all offenders have to do for ten years after being released.

Before I could think or react, he went on to say that he'd arranged for me to talk to the girl involved, who was prepared to tell me all about it. She was now in her twenties and he was still in contact with her. She would be able to prove that he was telling me the truth. He realised that this would be particularly hard for me, but he knew I would never believe he was a paedophile. However, in the meantime, the police were about to call me to make sure that I knew about the charges – particularly those of bigamy and failure to register his address.

He told me not to ask questions. The policeman would not be who he seemed to be, and there were other players at work here. He said they could only tell me certain facts, but if I asked questions they could highlight more and suck me in. He told me that Michelle had already had the police round and the house had been searched, but she was a professional and knew the score. I was to get rid of anything to do with her – any receipts from payments into her account, any reference, any information I had at all – because the police would come and search my property, too, and would arrest me for being complicit in the bigamy if they found anything.

I was really frightened now.

He said he could do time – that was acceptable – but without me the kids would go into care, and God knows what would happen to them then.

I destroyed everything I had: all the documents that I held referring to deposits made; the Company House reference I had found in 2000, listing Michelle's name as director of his company; the receipts for thousands and thousands of pounds paid into her bank account. I shredded and then burnt them as instructed before bagging the ashes and putting them in someone else's bin as I walked along the street, careful to check I wasn't being followed. When the policeman called me, I hid behind affected shock at what he was telling me – that my husband was a bigamist and paedophile. I already knew it was not true and, again as instructed, did not ask questions. The policeman told me his name was Peter and that he needed to tell me some rather difficult facts. He told me that Will had a criminal conviction for molesting a nine-year-old girl for several years, until she was thirteen. He also made sure that I knew he was being charged with bigamy and fraud, firearms offences and not registering his address. I told him that Will had only just phoned me and that I was too stunned and distressed to talk. That was true – but not for the reason that he thought.

As the police were aware that I had children, they had to inform social services and I was contacted by a social worker who wanted to meet me.

Suddenly all my doubts were gone. There was no way I could believe that Will was a paedophile. That was just not possible. Again, it reinforced my belief in him and the gulf between my two mental pathways widened. The alternative was not just uncomfortable; it was quite simply unacceptable and incomprehensible. He was my husband, my lover and my friend. He was the father of my children and I knew he was not capable of abusing a child.

I felt an immense loyalty to him, particularly because he was being victimised for having served the Western world all his working life but, for now, wanting a life of his own; he was being penalised for wanting out. It was all for us, all to protect us and to enable him to be home with us. It was all for me.

Will talked to me at length about the meeting with the social worker – how I should act and what I should say. I arrived for the meeting an hour early and wandered around the area looking for somewhere to wait. I eventually found somewhere dark enough for my mood and sat, slowly nursing a plain filter coffee. I was simply dreading the meeting ahead. How had I ended up here? Only a few years ago I was solvent, independent and confident. I had lived in a normal world with great friends and talked to everyone. Now I was alone and felt so lost. I still had friends but I didn't open up to them about what was happening. I felt trapped within a shell of silence; the only person I could talk to was under attack from forces I could not hope to defend him from.

I was completely out of my league.

When I arrived at the office it was very barren and rather shabby. There were plastic chairs and a pile of well-thumbed magazines detailing true-life stories of murder, deception and the inhumanity of the human race. I stared at the magazines and photos of ordinary people caught up in extraordinary situations. I have never bought these magazines or read them, and I was stunned to find that my life now resembled some of the stories advertised on the gaudy covers.

The social worker was friendly but cautious, and arrived with an enormously thick file that she carried in both arms. She took me into a small room with three office chairs and a radiator. There was no table and no other furniture. Again, I thought how barren and sparse it was.

I sat and listened as the woman told me that my husband was a convicted paedophile and that he had pleaded guilty to molesting a young girl from when she was just nine until she was thirteen. The child was called Anna, and Will was a friend of her family. Will had received a fifteen-month sentence in 1997 and was released after serving seven months. He had been assessed and was found to be unremorseful about his actions, showing little sympathy for the victim. The report stated there was a high risk of him reoffending. Despite this, when he came out of prison the family continued contact with him and he was allowed to spend time with both Anna and others in the household.

The social worker also talked about Will's other wife and family. She told me that they had five children together. *My God*, I thought. *Five children!* The social worker mentioned children from Michelle's previous marriage as well. I had no idea that Michelle had so many children, but it fitted with what Will had told me about her. I asked the social worker to tell me more of what was in the file, but she could only stick to what was publicly accessible, such as the court details of his criminal conviction, and details pertinent to my situation and my children.

I followed Will's advice. I hid behind a façade of shock, though I didn't really have to fake it. To hear these things and worse being said about a man you love is difficult, to say the least.

The social worker was patient and calm but couldn't fathom my reaction. Would I let him back in the house if he came back? I said I did not know. This had all happened ten years ago; I would need to hear his side of the story. She wanted to see me again and to meet the kids, to make sure they had not been molested. I told her I knew they had not been, but she was clearly unsure.

'He was never alone with them,' I told her, which was true. He was so rarely home that I never went out and left him there alone. I was always around with the children. He had never actually shown that much interest, and I usually engineered his physical play with them; I even had to ask him to talk to them on the phone when he called. He was a reserved man and, although he often told them he loved them, he was not particularly tactile with them; he never put them to bed or helped them get dressed. He was affectionate with me, but not particularly with the children.

'What about when you were asleep?' she said.

'I just didn't sleep that heavily when he was home,' I said. 'If he moved in bed, it would wake me up, because I was not used to having him in the bed with me.' Again, this was true.

'You can't know,' she said.

'I can,' I said.

I was molested when I was a young child by an acquaintance of my parents – a man who would play hide-and-seek with us and find me first. It was an innocent diversion with a hidden agenda. My molester made the experience into a secret game between the two of us, and at the time I did not know it was wrong. I was not aware that he was doing something harmful to me, nor was I armed with the language to tell anyone about it. The memories remained locked inside until I turned seventeen, when suddenly it all came blurting out. It took me a long time to come to terms with what had happened, and more specifically, how I felt about myself, because I had not thought it wrong at the time. Eventually, though, I realised I had a choice and chose to be a victim no longer.

So I gave my daughters sex education at the age of three – a simple, matter-of-fact, scientific, 'this is how it works' kind of talk. I told them that they could touch their own bottoms and wash between their legs themselves, but that no one else was to do so without their permission. I had done some research on the Internet and discovered that paedophiles do not molest children who can talk scientifically about sex, specifically because they can describe what has happened to them. When the paedophile first tests the waters (flashing his penis at the child, for instance), if the child says, 'That's your penis', they leave well alone – this kid would not make a good victim. The control and the molestation often depend on silence, and the child not having the words to explain or the knowledge to understand.

I had armed my children with language and knowledge to the extent that at the age of five, my eldest daughter Robyn asked her natural father and his new girlfriend, 'Daddy, do you put sperm inside Emma?' To which he choked and spluttered a garbled reply.

I had told my children that if any adult tried to touch them inappropriately – no matter who – that grown-up was being very bad. I had also said that if anyone ever told them there was something they were not to tell Mummy, then it should raise alarms. It meant that what the grown-up was doing was wrong, not them, and they must tell Mummy immediately – no matter who it was.

It astonishes me that we tell kids to be wary of strangers but not what the stranger might do, and why. The majority of people who are molested are abused by someone they know, not by a stranger, but still we shelter the children to the degree that they think they are doing something wrong when it happens.

I knew it had sunk in with my girls, because one day when my mother was babysitting she rang me in a fury saying Robyn (then four years old) would not let her wash her bottom in the bath. Even though my mum, a formidable force of a woman and someone Robyn trusted and respected, had insisted, Robyn had stood her ground and said, 'No, I do that.' I totally agreed with Robyn and told my mother so. I was so proud of my little girl.

So, I told the social worker that I knew they had not been touched. I did know, because I also silently knew my husband was a hero and would not do such a thing.

She told me that I would need to inform the social services if he came home, and that he was not to stay in the house.

I walked out of the social worker's office in an emotional daze. Numb and devastated, I not only felt out of my depth, I felt I was now drowning. I called Will as I walked down the road and told him what had been said about some of the information in the file. He sounded irritated and said, 'Yeah, that would be about right.' He told me that the girl was actually fourteen when she was asked to help out, and had signed a statement to confirm that she understood what was going on and what his work was. He reassured me and said that she was now in her twenties, and he would get her to talk to me on the phone that night to prove beyond doubt what he was saying.

The vital phone call was actually delayed, but a few days later he managed to arrange for the girl and I to speak and for her to send me a detailed statement about what had gone on. Will introduced the instruction to call in the middle of an instant messenger conversation and told me under no circumstances was I to use my real name.

I called her on the mobile number Will gave me. She told me her name and date of birth to verify who she was, and said that the statement she was sending right then was hers, and true.

I said, 'Thanks . . . thank you so much', and the call was over.

Then I went back to the computer and carried on the messenger conversation with Will. I asked him who Anna thought I was and he told me that she knew only that I was someone he was involved with who needed to know some more details about his past.

Then her statement came through:

> Hi,
> My name is Anna and I would like you to know that
> Bill has known me since I was nine. He has been
> good to me, though he was not around a lot of the

127

time because of the work he does with the govt (he says you've been told about that stuff . . .) and has helped out no matter who else has been around or what's been needed.

I always knew that someday this thing would come back up again and even though it was a long time ago, it is still really embarrassing for me to think about and talk about. We were all told what to say and we did what we were asked to do. All I know is that whatever it was for was a success and things were really good for a while after that. I don't know exactly what this is about but I do know enough that it's important for you to know that we were all just following the directions we had, there wasn't anything real in it and he's never been anything besides normal. We had to do a lot of interviews with the people in [Anna's area] after that, but since then we haven't had any more contact from any care workers.

I've agreed to do a quick webcam chat on Sunday night in case you need to know anything else and to let you see my face as well so you know who I am. Seriously, he's a great guy and never done any harm to me.

Hope that's all useful to you. A

If the girl herself could say that, then all was as Will said. The webcam chat did not happen, though, as I received an email from her saying that she was busy.

Now I had my proof but I could not tell anyone else, least of all the social-work department.

Meanwhile, Will was still facing jail and was wheeling and dealing to get certain charges removed – like those relating to fraud, which he kept repeating was just a misunderstanding. He had meetings with important people and told me that he'd been asked to do certain things in return for 'favours' in terms of reducing the charges. Will told me that his solicitor had suggested I write to the Crown Prosecution Service (CPS) in the hope that it would get them to drop the charge of bigamy. He was convinced that this would help. He drafted the letter, which he then asked me to send. It read:

> *My name is Mary Jordan (née Turner Thomson) and I am writing on behalf of William Jordan, who was arrested on suspicion of bigamy at Witney police station, Witney, Oxon and is due to report to Witney police station to be charged tomorrow.*
>
> *I feel that there are several things that the person making the decision to charge him should know in order to make a fair and balanced decision that will not hurt or penalise all those involved, any more than the actual revelation itself already has.*
>
> *It is important for me to say that while I am indeed the aggrieved party in this, I do not feel 'victimised' in the traditional sense of the word. While I was unaware of his marital state until this came to light, it is only fair to say that at the time of this offence being committed, there was an ongoing relationship between myself and Will and with a child suddenly on the way to consider, I can see how he may have felt considerable pressure to do what he did for the sake of legitimacy. While he has always 'worked away' from home (for reasons more obvious now than before . . .), he has always been a very loving and supportive father and 'husband', and to*

this day he continues to provide ongoing financial support to our family.

What I would ask you to consider is the effect of this charge on the children involved: the publicity and the stigma it will carry, both today and in the future, the impact upon his continued ability to provide for all involved, and the undoing of all that has been put into building their self-worth and self-esteem as children that are loved and cared for by two parents. I truly believe that all of this is punishment enough in and of itself and further action only penalises those of us who are truly innocent of any wrongdoing.

I queried it, saying that I was not pregnant when we got married; Eilidh had been born the February before, but Will said that it was the principle that mattered. By this stage, I just did as I was asked, printed off the letter on my letterhead and faxed it off.

I saw the social worker again, and again had to stall. This time she wanted me to make decisions about what to do; she wanted to come to my home and see if I was a fit mother.

Again, I was terrified and trapped. I could not and would not lose my kids, not for anything or anyone. I have never understood anyone who would put their husband before their children, and given a choice I would not do that.

Will told me it was harassment and they had no right to do this. He said I should see a lawyer and suggested I speak to one he had used in the past, one who knew he was an intelligence officer. He set up the appointment, but half an hour before the allotted time he rang to say he had given me the wrong contact and it was the wrong guy. I went anyway. I knew that a lawyer was bound by confidentiality and that I could finally talk to someone about this; I could finally break my silence and have someone understand.

The lawyer was brutal in the truest emotional sense of the word. I tried to articulate my situation for the first time in six years but I found it hard to break the conditioning, and therefore hard to say anything at all. I relayed the facts but could not remember or articulate why I knew certain things; I found it physically difficult to talk at all other than to describe the situation of the moment.

He told me flat. He'd heard it all before. He'd defended paedophiles and had heard everything from 'God told them to do it' to the 'intelligence officer' scam.

'But I have spoken to the people involved; I know who they are,' I said, desperate for some understanding.

'No,' he said. 'If he's been in a sex offenders' prison then he now has a ring of contacts and people who will help him. These people help each other set their victims up – that is how it works.'

I left the office stunned. I sat in the car and cried my heart out. I was beaten and heartbroken. Not because I believed the lawyer was right, or because anything had changed, but because a simple truth had emerged.

I believed Will, but I would leave him in an instant rather than lose my kids. If the world believed otherwise – the social workers and the lawyer – then I had to end the relationship anyway. I rang Will and told him so. It did not matter what the real situation was, the lawyer had told me that social services could take my children if I continued contact and a relationship with him; the lawyer had been very clear that I had no rights in the matter. I would not allow that to happen.

I felt devastated. 'They' had won.

Will did not agree and asked me to think about it. He said that social services had no right to take the kids and that he would go through the motions of counselling or whatever it took to keep the family together. We would get through this.

I was doubtful and upset. I could think no more and put it all on hold in my head. My sister Isobel was getting married the next day – 1 April 2006 – and it was my son's first birthday as well.

I needed to think about something else, and told him I needed a week to get my head together. His case was due to be heard on 5 April and we would see how that went. I would decide then.

For a few days, I tried to distract myself, occupying myself with my sister's wedding, trying hard to hide my misgivings about my own marriage. I used the event to focus on something other than my own situation and spent time with my kids and my family, knowing that very soon everything could change dramatically for us all. I tried to talk to my oldest sister, Lisa, who was home for the occasion, but found that I could not articulate what was going on and simply succeeded in worrying her about my mental state.

The celebrations over, everything hung in limbo as I waited for Will's court date. He had told me that two charges had been dropped, but those of bigamy and firearms possession stood. His court hearing was scheduled for 5 April 2006.

The day dawned at last, and I was dreading the phone call from his female lawyer. I busied myself, getting my three children ready to go out, keeping myself occupied and distracted.

Then the phone rang . . .

17

THE OTHER MRS JORDAN

5 April 2006

It was not the words, 'I am the other Mrs Jordan' that shook my world, but 'I was told *you* were an agent.' It was those seven words that finally bridged the gulf and made the reality clear.

In my head, I was transported across an unimaginable distance from one reality to another. I moved into another dimension, where my husband was not my husband; where my friend, my lover, had used and abused me for years; where the father of my children had lied to me and had risked my losing the children into care without hesitation – all to get what he wanted. This was now a new world where I had lived and loved the enemy; where a man I had known and loved simply did not exist.

All that from seven ordinary and rather small words.

◆ ◆ ◆

It was the afternoon of 5 April. I had been talking to my friend all day. My good friend who was a solid, wonderful, logical, caring woman with a life and problems of her own. She had known

Will and had strongly suspected something was not as it seemed, although she did not know precisely what. She had told me so years ago, but had also said that 'if' he was a conman, then he was 'a very good one'; and if I believed him, then she would support me. She had patiently waited for me to find out the truth, standing by me while the train slowly derailed, and was now ready to pick up the pieces. This was a true friend – one who had warned me but accepted that I had not heeded the warning, and I loved her for not judging me.

My friend did not react, or gasp or pity; she was solid and sure; she touched my hand and she listened – for how long I was really not aware. As we talked, in the back of my mind I could feel this other woman, this other wife, approaching, driving closer and getting nearer to the truth.

Will was texting me and panicking about my failure to answer the phone. I had texted to ask him what had happened in court, but he just said the case had been postponed. However, he wanted me to deposit another £500 into Michelle's account and said all hell was breaking loose; the charges being dropped depended on my fulfilling his request.

I ignored his texts, and when he called to find out why I had not done as he had asked, I used his trick of saying I had not received the messages and that my phone must not be working.

At around 5 p.m., Michelle arrived and I met her at my door. I was not ready to invite her into my home, so we went to the local cafe instead. It was a nice place, calm and with booths in which we could sit and not easily be overheard.

Here she was. His other wife, although part of me still did not believe it could be true.

Michelle is only five years older than me and a lot shorter. She had very long greying hair and it seemed to me that she had not looked after herself. I thought that it was something we had in common – weight gain through childbirth, or was it just a result of being kept miserable and alone? I tried to figure out when I had stopped caring about myself and my appearance. I had gained four stone in weight over the last five years and suddenly I was aware of my shape and my outward appearance.

I found Michelle was very forceful and organised. She seemed to have planned what to say and how this meeting would go. I was cautious and wary. Who could I believe?

She told me she had seven children, five with Will and two from her previous abusive marriage to a man who had indeed worked for the Pentagon in the US. She had been married to Bill, as she called him, since October 1992 and had weathered numerous affairs, including one while on holiday in Japan (he had not been there on an assignment, as he had stated) and one with a girl who had committed suicide a couple of years ago.

She told me that he'd had an affair with their children's nanny, and that this nanny had two children by him. One of them was four years old, less than a year older than our daughter and therefore conceived while I was pregnant and while Will was supposedly in Israel. Michelle also had a baby around the same time, which meant that all three of us had had babies within a year of each other.

I listened, still not sure what to believe. There was still a wall between Michelle and me; I was still conditioned not to trust anyone but Will. She showed me her marriage certificate and the children's passports, but I did not tell her that I had seen these exact documents before. Then she showed me the photographs of her children. One photograph of her seven-year-old daughter stopped me cold. This was my four-year-old daughter grown up; it could have been a photograph of my little girl. There was no doubt, nowhere to hide, no redemption. He was this girl's father, just as he was the father of my children, and he had lied to me from the very first email, with every breath.

Michelle told me he had a son in the US as well: a twenty-year-old boy by a girlfriend there. That brought the total number of children we knew of to ten so far. Five children with Michelle, one in the US, two with Michelle's nanny and two with me – this by the man who was infertile due to a 'bad case of mumps' as a child.

Michelle also told me that he was employed by the Ministry of Defence and worked for British intelligence. She knew this for a fact as she had lived that life for a long time. This was why she had thought I was another agent. On hearing this, the foundations of my belief crumbled. He was neither MOD nor CIA. Both of us were scared and did not know where to turn. I told her that he had proved to me he was CIA, but she knew he was not.

Michelle told me how she had MOD contacts that she had to talk to, including a man called 'Michael' with whom she communicated daily online. I told her that I had heard Will answer the phone saying he was Michael, but she did not believe me. She went on to say that 'Michael' could not be Bill because she would talk to him on the phone while online with Michael. She knew it was not him.

I kept trying to convince her that it was easily possible to do this, but she resisted. I could see now how my friend had tried to talk to me when I was still brainwashed – how gentle you had to be, how fragile that state is. Michelle told me how she had taken Bill back after he'd been to prison for sex offences; she'd not allowed him back immediately, but eventually she had let him come home – for the sake of the children and because she could not support the family alone. She knew that he had committed the crime but believed him when he said he was remorseful.

About three hours had now passed and I had to get back to my kids, while Michelle had to log in to speak to Michael. We went back to my house; my friend was still there, looking after my children.

Michelle met my children and I had to ask her not to talk about the subject in front of them. She commented on how all his kids looked alike, which was useful when trying to identify them. She looked into every part of my home. She wanted to see his side of the bed, his clothes and his stuff. She wanted to know what gifts he had given me and pointed out things that were 'his'.

At one point she waved at some shelves and said, 'Those are his books.'

But I had to correct her, saying, 'No, they are mine.'

She looked like she'd been slapped. 'You have much more in common with him than I do,' she said.

She talked to my friend, telling her some of what she had told me. But Michelle was still the one in control of the conversation. I was meek, subservient and shocked. I was led around my own home, opening up doors and cupboards so she could inspect my life and see where her husband had been. My friend had to go home and I left Michelle for a moment – the only moment I left her unwatched in my home – to say goodbye.

My friend took my arm and told me, 'Be careful – she has her own agenda.'

Michelle set up her laptop and went online, but Michael was not there. She called Bill and he answered instantly. Michelle talked to him and let me listen in on the conversation. She asked why Michael was not online and Will said he would sort it out.

Will was subservient to her, meek and compliant. It was a different relationship from the one he had with me.

Michelle phoned Bill several times that night and he answered each time. I called numerous times and was ignored. I got a text saying he was having a hard time because I had not deposited the money and he'd be in touch before the evening was over – he said

I should just hold on. Once, when Michelle called to say Michael had disappeared offline, Bill sounded as if he had been woken up and said he'd been in bed.

Michelle wanted to know about the money – where it had gone. She said he must be MOD because they paid the bills for his and her hire cars. I told her that he'd been using my credit cards for that. She wanted to see the statements and I showed her, although she still could not seem to get her head around this and kept going back to the fact that the MOD were paying for things for her family.

Michelle mentioned the time when he had come home with £15,000 in cash, and I knew that was from selling my home. She told me how he'd had all five kids in the car when he went to collect the money because they had nowhere to sleep, having been evicted once again. Apparently, the cloak-and-dagger approach he used that night, asking me to unlock the back door and stay inside in the dark, was simply to keep me indoors so I would not see his kids in the car and they would not see in. He left them for two hours outside my house in the middle of the night while he was inside with me.

She told me about the ways he had proved to her that he was who he said he was: times when he had told her about things that would come to pass in the news – MOD stuff. We talked about the details and about his driving and so on. Michelle also told me something extraordinary: she said that Will did not even have a driving licence. She said he had a provisional but not a full one, but somehow he managed to get away with speeding tickets all the time. He'd had around ten speeding tickets while I had known him, but always managed to make them 'go away' without consequences.

We talked through the night and nearly called the police together; I wish now that we had, but both of us were scared. There was more to this than just him – we both knew that. Michelle was particularly concerned about the money and how he was going to continue to support her children – to put them through college, for example. They had been going to private schools and she'd had a full-time nanny, even though she herself did not work. There was a stark contrast in our family lives: mine dependent on my mother for childcare so I could just keep our heads above water; hers involved big houses, private education and nannies.

She talked about schemes whereby she could control him financially, keeping him out of prison and working so that he could still support her. I could just see that everything was wrong; I had no plan for the future except to protect my children from any harm.

Michelle told me that he had taken her to London, where they had seen *Phantom of the Opera* and had also gone to the Japanese restaurant he had taken me to. It had been the first time he had seen it with her, too. She also called his parents and spoke to them, letting me listen to the conversation. Michelle told them she had discovered another affair and they said they were not happy with that kind of behaviour. They commented upon his 'nonsense', but they didn't seem to have any knowledge of me, and Michelle didn't say anything about the current situation. It certainly sounded like the same couple I had spoken to, but then how would I know?

Michelle kept on telling me more and more. She and Will had met in America and Will had actually been married to a woman called Alexis at the time. They had no children, and Alexis was apparently distraught when she discovered that Will had got Michelle pregnant. She had divorced him because of it. Michelle said that Alexis had become very successful since they'd split up, and had remarried. Michelle also told me that she was in contact with the ex-girlfriend with whom he had the twenty-year-old son and they were on good terms. Indeed, Will had talked to me about his childhood sweetheart called Devi, whom he had dated while they were at school together and with whom he had lost his virginity.

At 6 a.m., Michelle suddenly turned aggressive on me, putting her face inches from mine and telling me I had been stupid to fund him. It seemed to me that she was not far from the edge, and it even entered my mind that I could be in real physical danger. I wanted her to leave but I did not want to antagonise her. She was just another victim, but she had been brainwashed for sixteen years and I certainly felt that I could not trust her fully. I was not prepared to sleep with her in the house and I was suddenly very tired. I told her I had to rest and she started to pack up her stuff. We agreed that we would both leave Will/Bill and she asked me not to tell him we'd met, to give her a chance to get the kids away from him.

Michelle left, and I sat down on my bed.

PART TWO:
FACING REALITY AND
FINDING THE TRUTH

18

BEGINNING TO SEE THE LIGHT

6 April 2006

Alone for the first time since my world had changed, I sat in a vacuum. I had crossed the gulf and knew the truth. After the initial numbing shock, there was an overpowering emotion that can only be described as 'relief'. I was free. Free from fear of being followed or targeted by shadowy enemy agents – they were not real and no one was after me; free from social services threatening to take my children away from me, as now I could tell them the truth; free from my prison of silence and lies.

Over the previous five years, my life had often felt like that moment in a thriller when the lawyer of a murder suspect discovers a vital piece of evidence, such as a typewriter with a dodgy letter 'k' that makes her doubt everything her client has told her. The discovery of that one piece of evidence seems to prove beyond doubt that the situation is not what she had believed it to be; that the person she trusted is not who she thought. In the background, a chilling chord plays as the realisation hits and she suddenly knows the truth. But then the client comes back and demonstrates that all typewriters of that make have a dodgy 'k' and she's back where she started, sucked back in to believing again. At least now that would stop; at least the movie could end and I could have a normal life again.

I was in no way happy but I knew now what had really happened; it was all in the past and I could therefore put it behind me. I had a chance of happiness, as the future was mine and the children's to make for ourselves.

I sat for about half an hour like this, and then texted Will to tell him our relationship was over. I did not explain or elaborate, I just said:

> Been awake most of the night trying to work out what to do. I am not happy how things stand and have realised that you are not going to give me what I need or communicate in any reasonable or reliable manner. We have tried and tried to work things out and it is just not working. I guess we just make up too little of your life and it is not enough for me.

The answer I got back was brief and exasperated. Will claimed to have been up all night trying to keep one step ahead of the people to whom he owed money. He didn't appreciate my lack of support and seemed to think that I was just trying to provoke another argument. He said he had tried to explain the situation but that if I needed someone to blame for our predicament then I could go right ahead and blame him.

He clearly didn't think that I was serious about ending our relationship and over the next few days, he repeatedly tried to get in touch with me. He tried to call and I did not answer the phone; he texted and texted asking why I would not talk to him. He did not give up easily, or indeed at all, even though he discovered as soon as Michelle arrived home what had happened, because she told him everything immediately.

He continued to text me constantly and sent long emails explaining himself. He went through every tactic – fury at my failure to abide by his rules and contact him when Michelle called me; begging me not to leave him; indifference; trying to charm me; and then admitting what he had done and asking for forgiveness. He started to acknowledge certain lies: yes, the kids were his but they were not his real family – he would not under any circumstances explain this. Yes, the nanny had two children by him but that was an assignment. He tried every means possible to lure me back into his world and to get back into my head.

After a few days, I did talk to him on the phone again and asked him to explain himself, to tell me why he had done this. He just said there were reasons, but he could not explain on the phone; he repeatedly asked me to meet him, but I refused. I was scared of seeing him face to face: I knew his power was in eye contact and was frightened that I might succumb.

He did not take no for an answer and kept pushing me to meet up with him. At first, I was afraid that he would appear on the doorstep unannounced, but then I started to think more clearly and realised that he wouldn't. To arrive without being invited would immediately put me on the defensive, whereas if he was allowed to come, indeed if he was expected, then it would indicate that I was prepared to talk and wanted something from him; it would suggest that I believed he could give me answers and had hope that he would provide some sort of explanation for it all.

He continued to telephone and email, saying that he was not with Michelle any more, though she would also phone and ask if he had just called me as he had slipped out of the house.

On 1 May 2006, he wrote me a three-page email, once again telling me how important I was to him and begging me to reconsider.

He asked me whether I had given enough thought to the source of all the outrageous stories I had been hearing about him. Surely I could see that these were in part motivated by spite? What we had was truly special; we were destined to be together and he refused to believe that the intensity of feeling he had experienced had all been one-sided.

He played on the fact that I had once said I felt that I really knew him, the real man behind the mask; he said he was 'banking on that' and on the fact that once the shock of these untruthful revelations wore off, I would realise that this was still the case. If I held on to what I knew of him then we would somehow work our way through this mess. Above all, he said, I had to believe that he still loved me – this could never be denied.

He said: 'Know in your heart that I have always, always only ever tried to be the wind beneath your wings, to see you reach for all you have the potential to achieve, and to build your confidence and self-esteem to give you the courage to go for whatever you wished.' He claimed that while he was with me, life had new meaning; he had discovered a new purpose and a happiness that he had never experienced before.

Will refused to discuss what Michelle had told me, repeating that she had her own motives for saying what she did. There were explanations for everything but because of the legal situation he could not give them to me just now; I had to wait and it would all become clear: 'history would vindicate' him. He told me that he had genuinely thought when we met that he could not have children, but that he had lied about the reason. He said there were answers, but I did not believe him.

One evening in May, he called me on the phone sounding very drunk and, from the noise in the background, it also sounded as if he was driving. He said that he was sorry; that I really did deserve better than this. I asked him why he had done it; why the lies – why everything?

He said, 'Oh, Mary, I am just a bastard, don't you know that now?'

I asked what he had done with all the money and he promised he would tell me the next day – but he never did. It was just another way to keep me talking to him, a postponing tactic so he could find another route in.

It was terrifying, though, because each time he contacted me I could feel the pull; I could feel how easy it would be to believe him. But I would never go back to him regardless, because he was dangerous for both the children and me, from every angle conceivable – physically, emotionally and mentally.

I see-sawed back and forth in my mind, wondering if he had really fallen in love with me and then couldn't tell me he was already married. I would think that he did genuinely love me, then I would realise that he didn't; then he would contact me and I would believe that he did love me again. It was a horrible time, confusing and upsetting. The kids had it rough as well, because I was emotional and upset, but my friends and family rallied around to help. I do not remember much about those first few weeks, but I do remember that the further I moved away from the day I had met Michelle, the clearer my mind became.

In many ways, it was like emerging from a coma or coming round after hypnosis. How had he managed to manipulate me so much; how had I not been able to see what was going on?

Michelle phoned a lot and asked question after question, many of them seeking intimate details of my relationship with Will. It felt to me that she was demanding information as the wife talking to the compliant mistress, but I had not knowingly been a mistress; I had been his wife, too. I still was until he was found guilty of bigamy. I had to keep reminding myself that Michelle was also a victim in this.

At first, I automatically answered her questions. Was he still giving me money? she asked. 'No!' I said, astonished at her question.

He had never given me money. He had taken back all the money he had going through my account, leaving only a small amount to pay some of the credit-card debts and support the kids. But the credit cards were maxed out and constantly sucked dry by hire cars, cinema trips, rent and grocery shopping by Will. Now I knew the truth, I could see what the credit-card charges were for. In all, Will had put £129,000 into the business and had taken out £188,000. I had remortgaged my flat, raising £19,000 for him; let him take all the money he earned out of the business, and then sold my flat, raising over £105,000 capital for him. When that was gone, I had borrowed £18,000 from my family for him, and on top of that also supported our family, feeding the children and keeping a roof over our heads throughout the five years alone.

I was in over £56,000 of debt with loans and credit cards, because he had used the credit cards in my name to pay for another family or families, other women and alternative lives. Not only had all the earned income been taken, but also everything I had worked my whole life for. All to support his lies. After that, I was still left with the bills. In total, including the money he took from the business and from me personally, plus the debt he left me in, Will defrauded me of £198,000.

Initially, Michelle told me that she was trying to get away from Will, but pretty soon she seemed to have been sucked back into the story. The worst of it was that I could completely understand why, as she was exposed to him looking into her eyes and swearing to her that he was the only one she could trust – it was like being under a spell, and it was frightening to think of the power he'd had over me before. I could just imagine him telling her that she knew better than to believe this crazy story. He would have said, 'Think about it, Michelle, you know what I do; you know that there are reasons I would have had to have children with her.' I could imagine how she would have been made to feel guilty for contacting me, that she was responsible for their world falling apart and, although he would forgive her, she would be left feeling that she had betrayed him. She disappeared for a while and I tried, unsuccessfully, to contact her. I was worried where all this would end. I left it for a couple of weeks then I called her and she answered, sounding scared.

'I can't talk to you,' she whispered in desperate conspiratorial tones. 'Go back to the original story. What we thought at the start is true. It's all true!' She sounded terrified. 'I can't talk to you, I'll have to report this.'

'It's not real, Michelle; it's just Bill,' I said.

'No, you don't get it. You were set up, don't you understand? Think about it! You were set up to have kids with this man. His genetics and your connections!'

'What are you talking about?' I said.

'Think about it! Think about the times we live in, 9/11, think about who the enemy are. There are not enough mixed-race children going into the intelligence services!'

'Oh, Michelle, no.'

'I can't talk to you. I'll have to report this.'

I desperately wanted to help her but I knew there was nothing I could do. She seemed convinced that Will was a pawn in all of this rather than being in control, and I could fully understand why. He was that good, that clever at controlling people and persuading them that the fantastic story he was telling was the only possible explanation for the bizarre events unfolding around them. The challenge was on, and he was fighting to hold on to at least one of his victims.

Will told me that Michelle was just trying to get rid of me, as the competition, because she wanted all his money for herself and her children. He told me that she was all about money; he said that she knew he was in love with me and that I was all that mattered to him. I did not know what to believe, but realised that I could not depend on Michelle's story and I certainly did not trust Will.

◆ ◆ ◆

Quite a few months passed before I spoke to Michelle again, and by that time I was facing even more heartbreak at home. My mother had cancer and was undergoing chemotherapy. She had been ill for a year but had always played the issue down. I had been doing what I could to help and she stalwartly continued to socialise and refused to let anyone know she was losing her battle with non-Hodgkin lymphoma.

Over the summer, however, her condition worsened and she became considerably thinner, and more and more breathless. By July, it became clear that her illness was getting the better of her. As I had not been working, I spent a lot of time looking after her and taking her to her medical appointments – and because my father couldn't take it all in, I became the first port of call for her medical consultant.

On 7 August 2006, I was sitting in a cafe in stunned silence having just spoken to this consultant. I was staring into a large cup of coffee knowing that I had to phone my siblings and go to see my father. I was trying to work out how to tell them that my mother was dying and that she had days or possibly weeks to live, at best. My mother had been told but simply did not accept it; she told me she had to believe that she would get better. That was her way – always strong, always practical. I was going to miss her so much; she was such a big part of my life and my strength, particularly through this horrible time. At least she had seen me released from my prison, though; at least she knew I was on the road to recovery.

As I sat there, my mobile rang. I saw Michelle's number come up but answered before I had registered who it was. She aggressively launched into me, asking, 'Is he still giving you money?'

'What?' I said, very quietly.

'Money is still going missing; is he still giving you money?' she asked in an accusatory tone.

At last, I snapped out of my position of subservience to her. 'Michelle,' I said, 'I am not going to answer any more of your questions. I have just found out my mother is dying and I really do not want to do this any more. Why are you still giving him money? Why are you still with him?'

Her attitude, that I was some lowly mistress to be bullied, had finally got to me. I felt that Michelle had been manipulating me as well, in her own way. She did not think of me as a fellow victim but someone who had simply distracted her husband. She seemed to think it was totally unreasonable that he should even consider supporting the kids he'd had with me.

She faltered at the question. 'I'm not still with him; he's been taking money from the children.'

'Then get the children away from him,' I said.

She quickly said she had to go, and hung up.

But before that upsetting incident, I had been on a journey of discovery. After the first revelations about Will, I had a strong compulsion to learn more. I was certain that there would be other women who had been deceived by him and I badly wanted to save them. I called a few numbers from his old mobile phone bill, which I had been sent because it had been paid through the business. I spoke to a debt collector who had been trying to collect unpaid council tax on Michelle's house in Lancashire; another man who said he was a family friend but had had long chats with Will in the early hours of the morning; and then I called a number that was answered by a girl. She asked who I was, and I told her I was one of Will's wives. It was Anna, the girl he'd been convicted of molesting; the girl to whom I had briefly spoken and who had said she was sending me her statement to refute the abuse allegations against him.

Anna said that a lot made sense now. I asked her about her statement and she told me she had said what she'd been told to say on the phone – just as I had done on several occasions – but had not sent a statement. I told her that I had been molested as a child and tentatively asked her about it, but she simply said there was more to it than just that.

I spoke to Anna several times over the next couple of months. She tried to persuade me that Will was MOD, and she told me that she knew this because he'd taken her on to several air-force bases. She said he was desperate without me and was drinking heavily. She'd never seen him like this before. I tried to tell her it was all lies, that he wasn't who he said he was, but she would not believe me. I knew it was futile, but I had to try. I felt that Anna was the biggest victim in all of this, as she'd been abused and manipulated by this man as a child and was still being controlled even now. I felt desperate that I could not help her.

Later, when Will was in prison, I did talk to her again, and she was starting to get clear of him. She said she had been told what to tell me, about not being molested, about his work at the air-force bases and so on, by her MOD contact. I told her that this person was actually Will and she said she realised that now, adding that she had not heard from the contact since early September 2006, which was also when Will stopped getting in touch. Anna recognised what this man had been doing to her. She is an immensely strong person and clearly feels responsible for others. I believe she will weather the storm, and as long as she can rid herself of him and cut away I think she will survive. Like me, though, I do not know how she will ever trust anyone again.

I also contacted Alice – she had been a friend of Will's, but though he'd said he knew her through the service that was obviously not true. Maybe she had some answers that would help me. I sent an email to an old address, saying that I wanted to talk to her about unfinished business concerning Will. She called and we talked. The situation turned out to be very different from what I had anticipated.

19

ALICE'S STORY

Alice had not worked for the intelligence services, nor was she of a nervous disposition, as Will had told me. She is a cautious and articulate individual who had been taken in by Will as well.

Alice is a single mother with two older children and had met Will online in May 2005 – just a few days after he had picked up the servers following my move, and when he had first met our baby son.

Will's birthday is on 22 May, and he contacted her then, saying that it would make his fortieth birthday if she replied. He had wooed her the same way he had seduced me, and even arranged a date with her on my fortieth birthday – 5 June – but strangely enough, he did not show up. He begged forgiveness and claimed that pressures of work had delayed him, and Alice agreed to meet him again some other time.

They met and started to develop a relationship, moving fast into an intense long-distance liaison. Will told her that he worked in IT and that his sole contract was with a large software company. He claimed to have set up the company's UK office and had to work all over the UK and in Brussels for them.

Will and Alice met only a few times before he asked her for money. In June 2005, Will called her in a panic, saying that his car had been stolen and with it his credit cards and his laptop; all he had left was his mobile phone. He said that as he had not insured his laptop, he needed to buy a new one for work and was desperate. He was embarrassed, but could he borrow some money? She lent him the cash she had just received for selling her car to a friend, £4,500, which he promised to repay within a month. She also allowed him to use her credit card to pay a mobile-phone bill so that he could get back to work and out of trouble.

Will told Alice that he had set up a business with ten US citizens, all working on software contracts and MOD projects. He even told her that he'd been working on the digitisation of the CCTV footage of the 7/7 London bombings. Will told her when the information would be released to the press and what would be on the news before it duly appeared. Then he suggested that he get her a contract through his company. He offered to take her on in 'our' firm as an employee with an £800-a-week basic salary and a bonus of £4,000 every three months. Alice agreed and started working for him in July 2005. She sent her P45 to me about six times, believing I was the company's accountant and a close friend of Will's, but I never received it. Will gave her fax numbers and addresses but we still do not know what happened to the documents.

Will quickly asked Alice to move in with him and drove her to London, apparently to take her to his flat there – a flat that as far as we now know simply does not exist. However, on the way there he received a phone call demanding that he travel immediately to Brussels to deal with a legal issue he would have to fight for the software company. Alice had to stay with her cousin instead.

Alice had even housed the servers for a week in July while I was living with my parents; he had told her that there was no room in his office for them and spun her a story about it. He had picked them up from her one night before driving back up to Edinburgh to put them into my flat when I moved in there in August 2005.

Will told her that he had met a couple of people online and had dated two other women from the same dating site on which they'd met. Will had also taken her on trips to London. On one occasion, he had spent all day phoning her because the company accounts department, i.e. me, had put £1,200 into her account for him because there was a problem with his own. Alice was to take the money out in cash and drive with it to London, then they could go out to the theatre and have a nice evening together. He met her at Paddington Station and took her to a Japanese restaurant. She noticed that the waiters all smiled at him, and after hearing my story, she understood why. At the time, he told her he had taken at least one of his other dates there. He had his 'usual' very expensive teriyaki steak and drank champagne all night by the glass. Money seemed to be no object, but Alice ended up paying again because the money she'd brought for him was earmarked for something more pressing – he would, of course, pay her back 'soon'. They then went to see *Phantom of the Opera* and even the woman on the ticket desk seemed to recognise him. After the show, they went to another bar and Will started to tell Alice about his mother. She was very ill and he wanted to go back to the States to visit her. He asked Alice if she would go with him. She had not even had time to answer when Will got a phone call from his sister in the US telling him that his mother's heart operation the day before had been unsuccessful, and that they were going to operate again. Apparently, Will would have to find the money to pay for the surgery and send it over.

Will led Alice a merry dance after this, telling her story after story, including that he'd not been paid his expenses by the software company. Will asked, and Alice gave him more and more money. She got her £800 per week and passed most of it on to him after he had spun her various different tales. It sounds hard to believe but

I knew how he worked, how he managed to manipulate people. You'd only get your initial investment back (be that money, time or emotion) if you gave just this one bit more. He would say it was always just this once, and that this was the 'last time'. There was something strange about his ability to control, something neither of us could understand.

Although Alice got her £800 weekly payments, she did not get her payslips and no contract appeared; however, Will would still not let her call me. In all, Alice said, she'd given Will around £20,000, but by the end of August 2005 she was getting very suspicious of his behaviour and wanted to find out what was going on.

Will had asked her to move in with him again, and told her to meet him in a motel on the M25. She arrived and waited but he did not show up. She was there all weekend, phoning his number but getting no reply. Then on the Sunday morning, she called the company fax number, trying to get hold of me in order to ask if I knew where he was. My sister answered the phone because I was in London with Will, enjoying a weekend away, and she told Alice we were away in London. This spoke volumes to Alice, so she decided to do a bit of research for herself. She left a message asking me to call her back, and my sister phoned me. I, of course, told Will, who said he would deal with it while he went to fetch something from the car, and he called her, going mad at her. He told her that I was a very good friend and was not to be hassled due to her paranoia. He protested that he had been trying to get hold of her and that there must be something wrong with her phone.

◆ ◆ ◆

Will told Alice to continue waiting at the motel on the M25, but still did not show; eventually, on the Monday, she went back to her cousin's house, now practically broke.

Alice decided to google my name and found my old school website, which listed those who'd attended the twenty-year school reunion. I was on there as 'Mary Turner Thomson, now Mrs Mary Jordan'. She quizzed Will about this and he said that we were very good friends and that I sometimes found it useful to use his name and pretend we were married, although we were not. He then started to admit to her that I was somehow very well connected and it was due to my links with the powers that be, and even royalty, that enabled the ten US citizens to work for the company in the UK. If Alice were to rock the boat, then all ten workers, as well as their families, would be at risk of losing their jobs and homes and being sent back to the US. He was playing on her good nature, but by this time Alice was getting wise to him.

Alice went to her cousin, who was very supportive and took her to see an accountant friend of hers who worked with a large firm in the City. She explained her situation and was advised to set up a limited company for herself and try to pull away from Will; however, it was suggested that she finish the existing three-month contract before doing so. Alice had no money left, though, as she had given it all to Will – even her mortgage had not been paid and she was getting into serious debt.

In September 2005, Alice was still trying to extricate herself. She had changed bank accounts because she thought that the previous bank had kept making mistakes, allowing payments that were nothing to do with her. (She later found out that the errors had arisen because Will had been using her credit card details to pay for his car repairs, his contact lenses and for deliveries of grocery shopping to a 'friend'.) Then Will invited her out once more in London, and as he had once again not been paid his expenses, she paid for the meal by giving the waitress her new bank card. She then went to the ladies and when she returned the card was waiting for her on the table so that she could sign the slip. Alice never gave

Will her new card details or permission to use the card but, due to the events that followed, she later realised that this must have been when he took the details from it.

In October 2005, Alice finished her contract with Will's company, saying she had to look after her mother. Will was furious. By then, however, Alice was in serious trouble with her mortgage and credit-card companies. She made arrangements where she could and tried to work her way through her debts. Then, at the beginning of November 2005, she went to get some money from her bank account to give to her cousin and found that she had only £200 left, even though she had just been paid. She checked with the bank and they confirmed that £500 had been paid to Mercedes Benz in Oxford from her debit card. She was astonished but did not even have to think for a second before realising who had done it. The bank also said that her card had been used to make a payment of £1,000 to Mercedes in October and that two other attempts had been made to use her card at the same garage. They said that she would have to make a police report to get the money back, so she did exactly that.

The police asked Alice to keep Will talking to her until they could pick him up at the Mercedes garage. So Alice texted Will to say that the garage had called to let her know the car was ready. When Will arrived, the police were waiting and searched the car, finding papers pertaining to Mrs Michelle Jordan, along with the taser stun gun. But the vehicle was actually registered under the name of his other wife, Mrs Mary Jordan. Will was arrested on the spot, which was when he phoned me on his way to the police station, asking me to call the Office of the Deputy Prime Minister to say he would be late for work.

Alice filled in a lot of the blanks for me, as I did for her. Things started to make sense. However, we still had a lot of questions. Where had all the money gone and what had he been using it for?

Neither of us knew. Will had talked to Alice about other women he had been seeing that he had met online – maybe he had used it for them, but we suspected not.

Alice and I tried to get the customer-service team of the Internet dating site through which she had met him to cooperate and contact the other women he had met through their site. We were particularly concerned for those who had children, as he seemed to target single mothers – but they did not want to get involved. The only action they took to protect their customers was to remove Will's advert, and they would not try to warn the women he had already contacted.

Initially, during our long phone calls, Alice was nervous of me and apologetic for having had an affair with my husband. She believed that her actions had left me husbandless and my children fatherless, and I could hear in her voice that she felt guilty. I tried hard to explain to her that I was grateful – that she had set me free. It was her actions that had saved me, and my kids, from more harm. Yes, I was broke and on the verge of bankruptcy because of his debts, but I had all that mattered to me. I had my wonderful kids and I now knew the truth.

I will always be grateful to Alice for her actions and for the hours and hours she spent talking to me. She alone understood entirely and did not judge me for having believed Will. She alone knew how he worked and how he could manipulate people. Like me, she was looking back at the events and trying to understand how he had done this to us. I had found an ally, a friend, someone who had been through the same thing. Alice was another intelligent and honourable individual who had been honestly taken in.

I was silent and alone no more.

20

The First Wife and the Childhood Sweetheart

Bolstered by Alice's support, I wanted to know more, to find out where Will had come from and what had made him the way he was. I wanted information to fill the gap that he had left by taking so much from me. It became like an endless puzzle that I had to put together, knowing that I would never see every piece, but hoping that I might get an impression of the overall image if I found enough edges.

When she visited me at the house, Michelle had mentioned three people who might have answers for me. First, she said that Will had been married before to a woman called Alexis. Alexis had divorced Will in 1991, then remarried and moved on with her life. I wanted to find this woman, as I wanted to know that you did recover fully; that it was possible to have a life again. I also wanted to talk to someone who knew him before and knew his family. Michelle had been told that his mother had mental illness, but was it genetic? Were my children at risk? The only way to know was to ask. I did not want to call his parents, as I did not feel it was my place to disrupt their lives. Alexis, however, might be able to tell me.

I googled her name and discovered that she was a published author. There were several entries on the Web about her, so I sent her an email asking to talk to her regarding a personal matter relating to us both. She wrote back and I told her what had happened to me. She replied, and we talked at length. She told me her story and about their life together. There were so many similarities and so much more to know.

Second, Michelle had talked about Devi, who had been Will's childhood sweetheart and about whom I'd had pangs of jealousy in the early days when Will had spoken fondly of her and their youthful relationship. He had made them sound like the perfect high-school sweethearts; however, he had neglected to mention that they had a son together, probably because it did not fit with the whole 'I'm infertile' story. I wanted to find Devi as well as her son George, because again they might hold another piece of the puzzle.

It was Alice who uncovered the key to finding them when she mentioned that Will had a page on Myspace. I checked it out and discovered that he had only one friend on the site: his son George. The day after I found Will's page it was removed – but too late; I had contacted George and we were already talking. I communicated with George via email for some time and then in September 2006 told him that Will was on remand in jail. I also told him there was more to know, but I did not want to just blurt it out to him. George spoke to his mother and it was Devi who replied by email, very keen to hear what I had to say. We talked on the phone for a long time. Devi was another strong, independent woman with a great personality. But here was another devastating story.

So, bit by bit, Will's past came together. It was a story filled with dramatic events and it became clear that I was by no means the first victim of this man. There are still gaps but, as best as I can work it out from the people I have talked to, this is Will's story.

◆ ◆ ◆

According to Devi, she and Bill, as he called himself then, met when she started at his high school in New Jersey in 1980. He was fifteen and Devi was fourteen. They started dating almost immediately and were a couple on and off throughout the remaining years of school. Bill apparently kept ending the relationship and then starting it up again, over and over, keeping Devi off balance and confused. He would leave her waiting hours for a date and while Devi's mother would tell her not to bother, she always would. When he appeared, Bill would plead some family emergency and claim it was not really his fault.

Devi believed that Bill was jealous of her, particularly of her ability to save money. She really wasn't much of a spender, so whenever she had any she deposited it into her savings account.

Bill was already taking liberties with Devi. She knew that he had problems with his family and that his mother was ill. He told her that they did not have any food in the house and no way of getting any, so Devi gave him her ATM card, saying that if he needed $20 or $30 to get some emergency supplies for the family, that would be OK. The way the system worked in America at that time was that if you deposited money into an ATM in an envelope, the computer did not know how much was in it and trusted you to type in the correct amount. So you could deposit $20 and say it was $200. The bank would credit the account with that amount, making it immediately available to take out again. They would only realise the discrepancy when the envelopes were opened and the cash counted a couple of days later. Bill did just this several times over two days and took $600 out of Devi's account, putting her into overdraft. Devi was furious and ended the relationship. However, Bill wormed his way back over a period of time, and eventually they got back together again.

Devi had some problems with her parents and found herself homeless in 1983, so was living with Bill in secret in the basement of his parents' house. Bill's parents had never been keen on Devi, and as devout Catholics they would certainly not have allowed her to live in the house had they known she was there. But then later that year, Bill was convicted of writing bad cheques and was imprisoned, leaving Devi out on the streets.

Devi went to a priest for help and was sent to a cockroach-infested halfway house that had a reputation for being the 'worst place in the nation', as she put it. The other women threatened to beat her up on a daily basis and she lived in constant fear; she knew she had to get out for her own survival. It was clearly a horrendous time for her.

Devi did survive the experience, though, finding shelter in an abandoned building, and kept herself going. Months later, she bumped into Bill again, who said that he had been desperately searching for her since he had come out of prison. He said he had even had people looking for her and had reached the point where he thought she was dead. He fell upon her and declared his love, telling her how glad he was to see her. Devi was bowled over by this, as he really seemed to care about her. She did, however, get the impression that Bill was already in trouble again, though she did not know for what.

One day Bill took Devi for a drive, and when they got out of New Jersey he heaved a big sigh and said what a relief it was to be away. Somehow, though she cannot remember how, he persuaded her that they should just keep going, and they went straight on into Canada.

They lived rough for a while, sometimes in hostels and some-times on the street. They got money from churches to survive and scraped an existence. Then they saw an ad for a live-in position at a hostel in Barrie, Canada, run by an older German couple. For five days' work they could have seven days' room and board. They jumped at it and Devi learnt to sew fitted sheets and pillowcases, while Bill did wiring and construction work.

Bill did not feel content, though, and wanted more. He did not seem to understand that you get back out of life what you put into it. He resented having to work for a living and they argued about his attitude, because Devi believed strongly in the idea of 'a fair day's pay for a fair day's work' and she didn't feel that Bill was pulling his weight.

In 1985, Bill met a chap who offered them the same deal of working for board and lodgings, but in a chalet instead. By this time Devi was pregnant, and as she got larger she found it more and more difficult to work. Bill then found a couple who had a business, and for some reason they trusted him with a cheque for $500 which he kept for himself rather than providing the service they were expecting. The next thing Devi knew, the police were at the door, asking her questions. They asked her about a police shield/badge that they had found on Bill, and also a martial-arts throwing knife. Devi knew nothing about it. The police took Bill away and took Devi to a battered women's shelter very close to the prison he was in.

Devi tried to keep going and get babysitting work, but she was deported just two weeks before giving birth to her son in December 1985, going back to her parents in New Jersey. She was now nineteen years old.

For the next four years, from 1986 to 1990, Devi had no contact with Bill and did not try to find him. She found herself a job and started really getting her life together for her child.

In 1987, Bill was twenty-one and back in New Jersey starting a new relationship with Alexis, who was recuperating from surgery. Bill was very attentive to her during her recovery, bringing his guitar and singing to her. She quickly fell under his spell; within two or three months their relationship was in full swing and he had already moved into her home. It was then that she found out he had a criminal record for writing bad cheques, but she believed his explanation of how it had happened. He told Alexis that his mother had gone into hospital and he had been left to feed himself and his sister; he had wrongly thought there was money in the family bank account when there was not, and he paid the price.

Bill told Alexis that he owned a construction/heating and air-conditioning firm, so Alexis introduced him to contacts of hers and he got a contract to install a large office air-conditioning system. But Bill took the money for the purchase of the equipment and never did the job, instead appearing in a new car with no explanation for where the funds had come from. Too late, Alexis discovered that he was only a labourer in the construction firm. She was deeply embarrassed. But then Bill was arrested in 1988 and imprisoned again for nine months for writing thousands of dollars' worth of bad cheques. Alexis dutifully visited him in prison almost every weekend, taking him money and home-cooked food, even though it was several hours' drive away. He also called her on a regular basis from jail, running up her phone bill with reverse charges.

When Bill got out of prison, he went back to live with Alexis and they tried to conceive without success. Bill initially told her that he was estranged from his family but later introduced her to them. She knew that his mother was bipolar but did not know the extent of her illness. Bill's parents did not approve of his relationship with her, as she was older than him. Despite this, the couple were due to marry in 1989, but two days before the wedding Bill backed out, saying he'd changed his mind, leaving her again deeply embarrassed with guests already in town, a handmade designer silk gown hanging on the door and three bridesmaids all asking what had happened. Two months later, the couple entered the office of a justice of the peace and got married in private.

Bill now started to incur debts in her name. Each time Alexis caught him using cards without her permission, he would promise not to do it again. Although totally frustrated and angry, she tried to work on the relationship and keep Bill to his promises.

At the same time, Bill was trying to track Devi down, and he eventually found her in 1990. He told her that he'd had magnetic treatment on his head in Canada and was now a different man. However, although he swore he had changed, he claimed he still had the same love for her. He persuaded her again that she was his reason for living and that he wanted to have a relationship with her and their son. Bill even took Devi to see his parents and introduced them to George. After this meeting, they went off to an amusement park in Pennsylvania and Bill told her how happy he was that they were finally going to be a family. He bought her a ring and asked her to marry him.

Devi was understandably cautious, but he was so attentive and seemed so sincere. He told her that he was working in Washington DC, which explained why he was not around all the time; he asked her to g0 to Washington so that she could see the house he'd found for them. He told her to leave her job so they could set up home together. It took time, but Devi did eventually fall under his spell once more. This was a chance, after all, for their son to grow up with both parents at home.

It didn't take long, however, for subconscious alarm bells to start ringing – once, Devi picked up the phone to hear a woman named Alexis shouting at her, saying Bill was her husband. (Alexis does not remember this, but does recall finding a receipt in Bill's name for a woman's engagement ring and wedding band set.) Bill explained this by saying that Alexis was an old girlfriend who had sadly wanted more than he was able to offer, and was no longer mentally stable. Bill was so calm and matter-of-fact that Devi believed him. Another time, she called Bill's work and was told that he was out. She left a message saying she was Bill's fiancée, whereupon the secretary coughed and spluttered, 'You're his fiancée?' Devi thought it odd at the time, but did not realise the significance until later.

Devi left her job, as Bill had asked, and was supposed to go to Washington to see the house he'd found for them. Leaving George behind, she set off. Bill said he would meet her on the road; he told her where to wait for him – in the middle of nowhere. She arrived and waited for over an hour, but Bill didn't show. Devi realised that he wasn't coming, that he hadn't changed and was doing the same thing to her all over again – standing her up and leaving her waiting. She got back in her car and drove home to her son, furious beyond belief at being played by him again.

Devi got her job back and got on with her life again. It is one thing to mess a woman around, but it is a totally different thing to play with the life and affections of the woman's child as well. Although determined never to see Bill again, this was not the end of her story. The year 1990 seems to have been a busy one for Bill. Not only was he newly married to Alexis, but she discovered that he was having an affair with a Hispanic cleaning woman at work. Then it came to light that he was having affairs with two other women as well, one of whom, Devi, had already borne him a child and one who was pregnant, Michelle.

While this was all going on, Bill and Alexis started to go to counselling to try to save their marriage. Alexis was tired of his lies and of his disrespect for her, but she had made a commitment to him and wanted to make it work. The counsellor initially thought that Bill was mentally ill, diagnosing multiple-personality disorder; however, he later said that this could have been faked. After the initial diagnosis, Bill started to talk to himself in different voices in front of Alexis – one would be aggressive and call the other character 'milk toast and spineless'. However, it was the milk-toast character that Alexis was in love with. Things deteriorated between them and Alexis became wary of being alone with him when he was doing this. She thought he was having a mental breakdown and that he might be dangerous.

Alexis finally lost patience with Bill due to his unfulfilled promises to stop incurring debt, as well as his behaviour in general, and took him to court. She came to the conclusion that he was not mentally ill at all but simply using any tactic he could to manipulate her. Bill was ordered by the judge to pay off the debts monthly but he just ignored it, so Alexis took him back to court and he was imprisoned again. Alexis told me it was Michelle who bailed him out; he moved in with her.

In 1991, Alexis divorced Bill and closed the door on her life with him, leaving the house that they had shared and moving into a condo. She took in a roommate to help with expenses that had accrued during their marriage. Meanwhile, Bill and Michelle moved to the UK to be married in Lancashire in October 1992 – by which time she was already pregnant with their second child.

In 1997, Bill went to prison and served seven months of a fifteen-month sentence, having pleaded guilty to sexual offences against a girl under the age of thirteen. The girl had written in a diary about her relief that he was no longer showing her attention, and it highlighted the issue to her mother, who went to the police.

Michelle was pregnant again by Bill and their third child was born just after he came out of prison.

By 1998, as far as I understand from Michelle, Bill was back with her family and had changed his name from Bill to Will, though Michelle said that she never called him Will; he was Bill at home and Will in business. This was also when they took on a new nanny to help with the children.

I discovered that in late 1998, Will started pursuing a single mother called Helen, with whom he was working in Surrey. He spent a lot of time visiting her office and wooing her, repeatedly asking her out. Helen found this very flattering, as he was extremely attentive, apparently younger than her and had a certain exotic appeal. He was very persistent and ultimately she succumbed to his advances and agreed to go out with him. So they started a fling, as she would describe it, although he would repeatedly disappear. Despite taking oral contraception, Helen fell pregnant in early 1999. This came as a considerable shock to her as she was already a single mother and felt that life was difficult enough. Almost immediately, Will started to disappear more and more frequently, while continuing to talk about being there to support her and her child.

Around this time, Helen was starting to become aware that Will had the capacity to tell different stories to different people. For example, although he had told her that his father was holding down three jobs to support his ailing mother, she overheard him telling her friend that his father was an eminent cardiac surgeon!

Helen continued to grow increasingly suspicious of his behaviour, especially as he was very evasive when asked if he was going to tell his parents that they had a grandchild on the way. He repeatedly found excuses not to call them, but Helen's growing unease led her to investigate herself. Luckily, Will had inadvertently disclosed his parents' contact details in the US in an application to rent a 'family' home for himself, Helen and the children. So she called them and it quickly became apparent that they knew nothing about her or the current situation. Helen and her friend confronted Will, who was annoyed at Helen for calling his parents. Having clearly been found out, he simply shrugged it off and walked out, never to be seen again.

Helen was heavily pregnant when Will disappeared from her life and to this day he has never met his child. This might not sound very shocking or out of the ordinary in today's world, but at that time and on a personal level the implications were immense. How was she going to cope with a newborn child? How was she going to explain to her older children that Will had just disappeared? How was she going to hold down her job and keep everything together?

It did obviously change her life, but Helen is very robust and has continued to support and successfully raise her children.

By the year 2000, Will had set up the company of which Michelle was director, with her address listed as their house in Lancashire, but had moved the family to Gullane, just outside Edinburgh in Scotland. Will had pursued the nanny, saying his marriage was on the rocks and that he was in love with her. She resisted for some time but eventually succumbed to his charm, falling pregnant in June 2000. He was working out of a serviced office complex in St Andrew Square, which is where I met him for our first lunch date. In November 2000, Michelle was again three months pregnant and their nanny was five months pregnant. It was at this point that he started emailing me, saying that he felt it was only fair to warn me that he could not have children of his own.

The nanny's baby was born in March 2001 and Michelle's fifth child with Bill was born in June 2001, by which time I was also pregnant and we were planning our wedding.

Will disappeared out of my life in July 2001, apparently going to the troubled areas in Israel and the Palestinian territories; however, while he was 'abroad', the nanny fell pregnant again.

When Will told me the operations base in Gullane had been moved, the truth of the matter was that the Jordan family had moved back to their house in Lancashire. This was also around the time that Michelle contacted Devi, wanting to talk. Michelle told Devi the whole story: how they now had five children together; how he had got the nanny pregnant – twice – and that he was now working for the Ministry of Defence in the UK. Michelle wanted her children and Devi's son to get to know one another, for her kids to know their older brother. Devi was suspicious, though, and did not know what to think. However, shortly afterwards she was contacted again, this time by Bill. He acknowledged that he did indeed have children with Michelle, but that they were divorced now. He felt very uncomfortable about it, and told Devi that Michelle was not mentally stable. Having opened the door again, Bill said that he wanted to start giving her and George money and he begged to be able to meet his sixteen-year-old son. He asked Devi to bring him over to London, and she agreed because she knew how much George wanted to meet his father. They planned the trip for later on that year, in 2002.

In February 2002, I gave birth to our daughter Eilidh and only three months later the nanny gave birth to their second child. Will met Eilidh in May 2002, after coming back from the Jenin massacre a haggard man, thin and pale, with his feet mangled, wanting out of the CIA in order to dedicate himself to his family.

Meanwhile, also in May 2002, Bill paid for a fortnight in a luxury Knightsbridge flat within walking distance of Harrods, and was supposed to spend time with Devi and George. However, he had to keep coming and going, so Devi and George just enjoyed London together. Bill did not pay for anything while they were there, although he tried, unsuccessfully, to persuade Devi to tell George that he had. Bill told her that he was now working for British intelligence and he had physical evidence of this in the form of envelopes addressed to him with the MOD as return address and letters bearing the MOD logo. Initially, she believed him, but she did not fall back into a relationship with him.

For Devi, this trip was about her son meeting the father he knew nothing about. When they went home, Devi thought about it and realised that his story about the British intelligence work was probably not true and the evidence fabricated, but her son was intrigued.

At the time of their trip in May/June 2002, Bill had two babies in his family home – one with Michelle and one with the nanny – as well as our own baby daughter Eilidh, whom he met around the same time. No wonder he looked so tired and haggard when he returned home to me.

That was the 'last of Bill', as Devi put it. He is behind her now and she is free of him. He has periodically contacted George, which has worried her greatly. George is naturally curious about his father and Will is just as smooth at manipulating men as he is women. It is easy for a father to say to a son that their mother is just bitter – that the story has been twisted by emotion – and it is natural for a child to believe both parents to be basically good. It is another thing when the son hears the same story of his father's shocking behaviour from the subsequent mothers of his paternal half-siblings.

George was in just as much danger as the rest of us, in some ways more so, and Devi was grateful that I had let them know what was going on, because suddenly George got a wake-up call. Every child looks up to his or her father regardless of what he has done, and Devi did not want him to follow in his dad's footsteps.

She found it hard, however, to explain to George why not. Now he had a clearer picture of what had really gone on, and hopefully that will make it much harder for Bill/Will to manipulate him into helping with his schemes. Devi also hopes that it will ensure that George recognises his own behaviour and does not fall into the trap of expecting more than he puts into life, or leaving people waiting around for things that he has promised.

Devi is an amazing character and I loved talking to her on the phone. She made me laugh with her turns of phrase and I have the utmost respect for her. She is certainly not meek, subservient or gullible, and proved to me once again that this man does not choose easy targets for his manipulations. The name Devi means goddess in Hindu culture and, considering her strength and determination to overcome life's hurdles, it is a fitting name for her.

Alexis and I still write to each other, and she is another caring and supportive woman. Intelligent and articulate, she is well past the hurt that Bill caused her and showed me the compassion that can come only from someone who has been through the same hurt and is stronger for it. She is the first Mrs Jordan, as far as we know, but is now happy and has moved on. She wrote to me:

> *I say that we have much in common because I can see myself in you. Not only did Bill take advantage of me, but also of my family, friends, and my religious organisation. He assumes whatever identity or persona that is necessary to carry out his plan.*
>
> *I am amazed about the similarity in our wedding stories. The only difference is that I was not pregnant, but I was trying!!!! You and I both were given an opportunity in life to walk away when the weddings fell through – yet we both walked head on into it when the time next presented itself again. I am not sorry that I did because the entire ordeal enabled me to grow tremendously. It taught me a lot about people and it taught me to choose more carefully and to love myself more. It, of course, takes time to come to these conclusions. I see the whole situation as quite a bit of bad karma that needed to happen so that I could clear it out of my life so that I could become truly happy.*
>
> *You also asked me how I got over him and moved forward with my life. I used my faith to help me gain strength and wisdom to see the facts clearly and to believe what I was seeing (although my heart*

wanted to believe something other than the truth).
It did not take long for me to grasp the reality of
the true essence of the man that I had married. I
was not interested in meeting or marrying anyone
else after my ordeal with Bill. I believed that men
were such liars and I did not trust anything that
they said after the Bill experience. Then a girlfriend
of mine introduced me to my current husband by
phone. Well, who knew that it would be this man
who would help to restore my faith in the goodness
of another human being. He was and is the kind of
man who says what he will do and does what he says.
He is one of the most trustworthy people that I know.
It took me several years, however, to be able to trust a
man again. I gave my poor husband hell for a time!
Then I started to realize deep inside that he was not
Bill and that I had changed the karma that I had in
my life to choose so poorly. I now had the fortune to
attract a different kind of man. Also, when I realized
that I did not need to have a man in my life to be
happy, everything came together.

You said you'd been told both Bill and I were
CIA agents and that our marriage was a cover. That
is so untrue. Neither of us have ever been a part of
the CIA. At least I know that I have not and I seri-
ously doubt that Bill/Will has been. He's been in jail
too much!

Alexis was a breath of fresh air. I was so grateful for her words of
wisdom and also for the knowledge that not only was I now not
alone, I was actually in the company of many. He had done this for
over twenty years and had practised and perfected his techniques

over time and through experience with others. This is why he is so good at what he does – the predator, the hunter, the psychopath. (I looked up the term 'psychopath' and it was unnerving how accurately the behaviour described my erstwhile loving husband.)

Alexis told me that Bill had burnt all his bridges in the US; that all the government services were now linked; and it would be impossible for him to practise his art over there any more. That was probably why he was over in the UK – our systems are simply not linked up, especially across the borders. When I married Will, I automatically expected the registry office to check he was not married to anyone else – that is what you pay the registration fee for. It was not a conscious thought, just an assumption made in hindsight. However, it turns out that in Scotland they only check the registrations in Scotland, and in England the English ones and so on. So it seems to be easy to slip through the net.

Alexis and I chatted like old friends and had much in common – we could now recognise the many broken promises and wasted opportunities, the times we had not seen the truth and had fallen for his charm. So much had been lost, but that was behind us and we could look to the future; we had both learnt so much – the hard way.

She was calm and relaxed. Happy. She gave me hope, and confirmed that I was on the right path.

After *The Bigamist* was published, other women came forward to tell their stories about their involvement with Will Jordan. One woman called Karen met him via online dating and got engaged to him in November 2004. This was just as I ran out of money from the sale of my flat and was five months pregnant with Zach. She was another single mother to whom Will quickly proposed. He told her that he wanted to try for a baby but she didn't stop taking the pill, so did not conceive.

In March 2005, Karen got fed up with broken promises. She went through his pockets and found an envelope addressed to Mr and Mrs Jordan. She wrote to Mrs Jordan and ended her engagement to Will. However, the address she had was one neither Michelle nor I recognise.

I learned of another victim who met Will in 2005. Just after Will got himself a contract with the Office of the Deputy Prime Minister and had started Alice working for 'his' company, he contacted another woman over the Internet – Holli, a twenty-seven-year-old recent divorcee with two children. As I listened to her story, I realised that it had an extremely familiar ring to it.

Will told Holli that he was thirty-three, and that he was John Prescott's right-hand man. Indeed, he had taken her into the ODPM offices to show her around – waving to the security guards and talking familiarly with them. He swept her off her feet, moving swiftly into a relationship with her. He spent time with her family and talked about commitment and moving in together. He even bought a new suit to attend a big family event with her.

Holli thought she had 'struck gold' and that life was on the up. She said he was 'very attentive and a complete natural with my children', and at the time she felt this was 'incredible, as he claimed he had no children of his own because he was physically incapable of fathering'. Will was particularly fond of Holli's daughter and was bonding well with her, helping her pick out bedroom furniture and other items for their new home together. Will wanted Holli to marry him in America, for them to live in her dream home and be together forever. They had fantastic times throughout the first four months of their relationship, up until November 2005 – at which point he was arrested for using Alice's credit card. He took her to London and they had a particularly lovely evening at *Phantom of the Opera* and a superb meal in a Japanese restaurant. Holli told me that Will did have a habit of disappearing and once told her, after vanishing for five days, that he had been to America as his mother and father had been involved in a horrific car accident.

Will pressurised Holli into ending her tenancy agreement with her landlord so that they could move in together. He would not put the deposit down on the new house until she had committed herself. She did, and he put a £1,000 deposit down on a four-bedroom property in her home town. Holli also had to leave her job, as they would be moving too far away from where she worked. However, when it came to signing the new lease in early December, Will was nowhere to be found and Holli wisely would not sign it without him. She had to put all her belongings in storage, moving her small family into bed-and-breakfast accommodation for three months until she could make new arrangements.

Will vanished out of her life only to reappear again briefly in January 2006, saying that they could now 'really start living'. But then he disappeared for good. Holli only recently learned of the court case and his conviction and says, 'I am now a much stronger person, and a superb judge of character, I hope, through a lesson being learnt the extreme hard way.'

21

BUSINESS AND OTHER CONTACTS

In the course of our conversations, Alice and I started to dig a little further and to find out more and more about Will's activities. We uncovered numerous sources who told us of the damage he had done to people in business. After going through the credit-card statements, I called the firms to which he had made regular payments and came across companies that he was supposedly doing work for up until 2003. He had been paid for contracts that were never completed, and had been refunding people for work he had been paid for but not finished – on my credit!

Two people I contacted were very eager to talk to me and reveal the extent to which he had ripped them off. Apparently Will had undertaken contracts for programming code for their websites and so on – and for several months had been paid for the work, but never produced the results. He kept putting them off and telling them it was on the way, while still accepting payment.

I found one chap called Malcolm who told me that he had been so frustrated with Will's failure to deliver that he had on several occasions visited his home in an attempt to force him back to work. Having failed on all fronts, he asked another programmer to check out the sections of work Will had done. He was told that the databases were twenty years out of date and there were glaring holes in the code, which any decent coder would not have made. At that point, Malcolm came to the conclusion that Will had only one skill: he could talk a good talk. He then tried to find out more and talked to other companies that Will had mentioned on his curriculum vitae. He uncovered a trail of devastation; he'd worked out that Will owed around £115,000 for work not carried out. Will had worked for this chap around 2002–03, developing a cinema database and network operating system. Strangely enough, this was the same cinema complex that Will had told me he owned at one point. He had even shown me photographs of the place and told me that he was due to be paid about £100,000 for his share when the complex was sold. As always, the money had failed to materialise; according to Will, it was just another of the 'assets' that the CIA took back.

Interestingly, Malcolm told me that he had paid Will a few lump sums, and felt sorry for him because Will had said his wife had cancer and needed treatment in London. Malcolm had even agreed to pay for an apartment for a week so that Will could take his wife down there for treatment. He was furious when he discovered that Will had actually booked two weeks in a luxury apartment in Knightsbridge! That was in May/June 2002, and it was not Michelle that Will took there but Devi and their son George. I was also told that Will used this 'cancer' trick to get various other lump sums out of Malcolm's business.

Malcolm also told me that Will often stood him up. On one occasion, 26–28 October 2003, Malcolm was kept waiting at a hotel in Lancashire. Will was on the train but it had been delayed, then stopped. He'd be there in the morning, in a few hours, etc. At the same time, Michelle was waiting for Will and was getting similar messages. However, Will was on honeymoon with me at Shieldhill Castle.

Eventually I got up the courage to phone a friend that Will had talked about on several occasions. This was a chap called Jonny, who worked in Malcolm's cinema when Will was there and had known him for several years. We had a long chat about Will and he told me he had been an OK friend; though he often disappeared for long stretches, Will would stay in contact with him and usually answered texts. He had not heard from Will for about six months. Jonny told me that Will hadn't taken a lot of money from him, apart from just under £1,000 for paying off the bailiffs when they were at the door. He said that this seemed to be a regular occurrence and that Will always seemed to be short of cash, despite always driving new cars. Jonny would feed him whenever they were working together because Will never had money to buy food. On one rare occasion in 2003 when Will was carless, Jonny even bought him a second-hand Daewoo, though I have no idea what Will did with it. Jonny did not know about me or about the other children, though Will had told him he had a grown-up daughter in the US. He also talked about how the owner of the cinema had given Will a £25,000 advance when he told him that his wife had cancer and needed treatment. Will had apparently told Jonny that he had previously been in business and had lost everything when 9/11 destroyed his biggest client; he was just trying to get it all back again.

People were happy to talk to me and often eager to find out what Will had been doing. The business people told me that Will was indeed not a good coder or programmer, and that when they checked the databases he had created they often had fatal flaws. His amazing abilities in computer technology were another blatant lie; again, just a confidence trick. He was always so convincing – I had just taken it for granted that he knew what he was doing. Suddenly my fears dissipated and I felt more secure in my home – I had been worried that it might be bugged and my computer continuously monitored.

I found people in Lancashire who had known the Jordans since they moved to the UK in the 1990s. They told me the family had been hounded by debt collectors from the very beginning. Their old neighbours told me how they had received a package through the post one day that contained five sheets of paper on which were repeatedly written: 'Will Jordan is having intercourse with my daughter.' They could only assume it had been sent to the wrong address and was meant for Michelle. They told me how the family moved out and back in several times – always moving at night. Michelle had told them that Will was working with the government, but never actually explained what he was doing. Then the nanny left and they met her with a child that looked remarkably like Will. Initially, I thought that this was the same nanny who had been pregnant in Gullane, but they told me that the child was at least ten years old when they had last seen her recently, so it could not have been the same one.

Alice got on to the directory website www.192.com and told them the story of what had happened to us and they gave her all the help they could offer, which was a wonderful thing to do. So she researched data files on the Internet and found birth certificates with Will listed as the father. We found a listing for the nanny who'd had two little girls with him within two years, it seems. One was born in 2001 and one in April 2002 – meaning that they are very close together and either side of my daughter, born in February 2002. This was more proof that Will was not away in the Palestinian territories while I was pregnant with Eilidh.

Alice found the Gullane nanny's address on www.192.com and I wrote to her in early November 2006, telling her who I was and including photographs so that she could see that Will had been part of our family. I told her that I would like to speak to her and received a phone call very shortly afterwards. We talked for about an hour, and she was very hesitant. I reassured her and told her my story: how Will had met me and wooed me; how he had convinced me he was CIA; how I visited the house in Gullane and had been told it was an operations house; the lies, the stories, the fear, and the way he had drained me of money. She listened and I did not ask her questions. I told her about Alice and how she and I had found comfort in each other and in finding out more of the truth. She was cautious and said she needed time to come around, but hopefully one day she will tell us her story. In the meantime, she wants to remain silent; she is confused by all this and I understand that.

I had the constant desire to call Will's family, to find out more about these people who were supposed to be my relations, too. The mother and father-in-law who had allegedly come over for our engagement party but who never showed up. The people I had spoken to on the phone, who had been so welcoming and so happy that Will had finally found someone to settle down with. I wanted to know absolutely that they were not involved with what he did; that the people I had spoken to were actors he had hired, or something like that. I wanted them to know they had other grandchildren, but I knew I could not call them; after all, they are his parents, not mine. I desperately wanted to know more about his past, though – to find some reason behind all this.

Eventually, seven months after meeting Michelle and living with the knowledge of what had happened to me, I plucked up the courage to call Will's sister in the US. I was nervous and felt incredible trepidation in doing this, as I was not keen to disrupt someone's family, but I could not think of any other person who could possibly help me. I hesitated, then dialled the number.

Initially I talked to someone in Will's sister's house who asked what I was calling about. I told her that I was one of her sisters-in-law and that I was married to Will Jordan. The person quizzed me, and in my discomfort I told her that Will was in prison. She said to me that her father was also in prison and I stopped cold. 'How old are you?' I asked, and the girl answered, 'Nearly fourteen.'

I was shocked, as I had thought she was a lot older – I suppose my experience is with much younger children and it hadn't dawned on me that I wasn't talking to an adult. I got tongue-tied and embarrassed. The girl gave me her mother's email address and I said I would email her some photos so that she could see who I was, and rang off.

About 1 a.m. I got a call back and I spoke to my sister-in-law for the first time. She was angry with me for telling her daughter so much, and I apologised over and over. I knew that I had done the wrong thing, that I should not have called, but she was kind to me and understood that it had not been intentional. I realise now that it was selfish of me to contact Will's sister that way and that it was too much to expect answers from her. She was shocked by what I told her and upset by the story. She did not seem close to Will, but it was still a lot for her to take in. She did not even seem that surprised, although I imagine there was a lot that she did not say. I had emailed her photographs of our family and our wedding day, so she knew I was not lying about being married to Will. She asked me to let her know what happened with the trial, but was not keen to continue contact otherwise – which I understood and accepted.

22

THE POLICE

Over time, yet more came out about Will. He had rented a million-pound house in Oxford for Michelle and the children but had not paid the rent on this for several months. This was where he had been staying when he had told me he was living in his car. I remembered angrily all the nights I had worried about him out there in the cold, the blankets I had bought him because he told me how miserable it was, and how I was made to feel guilty because at least I had a roof over my head. It was all nonsense.

I knew who the landlords were, as I had once paid the rent myself (although at the time I had not known what the payment was for) on Will's instructions. The landlords pressed charges for four months of unpaid rent, but twelve hours before the awaited hearing Will walked into the court asking for a postponement. He was awarded another month, which allowed the family to stay in the house for a further month rent-free.

Eventually Will did get taken to court for £13,000 unpaid rent and he calmly told the judge that he had £11,000 in the bank and was just waiting for a cheque to clear. The judge, extraordinarily, awarded him another week, rather than demanding he pay the £11,000 there and then – much to the frustration and annoyance of the landlords, who would lose even more money as a result. But eventually Will and his family were evicted.

I discovered that Will had managed to rent the house based on his references as right-hand man to John Prescott – he had been working as an IT contractor for the Office of the Deputy Prime Minister at the time, so I suppose it must have been quite easy to write himself a reference. The landlords are still incredibly frustrated with the legal system, as it seemed to allow a conman to drag the process out for his own convenience. They are also furious about the system for checking tenants' references, as it failed to highlight that Will had numerous county court judgments against him for non-payment of rent.

When the bailiffs arrived to evict them, Will was apparently overseeing the removal of the family's furniture and belongings into the back of a van. The removal men dropped his grand piano while they were there, to the amusement of the landlords. This news irritated me greatly, as why had I been forced to sell my life-insurance policy when he had a grand piano he could have sold? I later heard that the company from which he had hired it were looking for him, as they wanted it back.

Will's first court hearing for the bigamy and fraud charges was scheduled for 5 April 2006 – the day I had been expecting to receive a call from his lawyer, but instead received a call from Michelle. It was, however, postponed. The case was scheduled to be heard in the magistrate's court in April, May and June and each time it was postponed. Finally, in July, it was referred up to the Crown court, but they in turn put it on reserve four or five times. Each time I was given a date I thought I could see an end to this torturous ambiguity, only to be disappointed again. Until the case was tried I was still 'married'; when he pleaded guilty I would be 'illegally married'; then I would have to take it to civil court and get my marriage annulled or voided at the registry office – at which point I would become 'single' and never have been married at all. Strange system we live under.

Until then I was living in limbo. When I had to fill in forms for the DSS or other official organisations, I found that I couldn't tick any of the boxes: 'married / separated / divorced / widowed / single'. Only once did I come across a box for 'other' – I guess bigamy happens so rarely that it is just not taken into consideration.

During the summer, I talked to the police in Oxford and told them what had happened to me, but they did not seem all that interested. They had my marriage certificate and that was all they needed. They did not need me to act as a witness, even though I told them how he had controlled me and taken everything. I even told them about the letter he had me send to the CPS, but they did not seem to think that it mattered very much. They suggested that I talk to the Scottish police if I felt I had a case, but it was not pertinent to their investigations in Oxford.

In August 2006, I contacted the CPS myself and asked what they intended to do with the letter that Will had had me send to them. They told me that as he planned to plead guilty to the bigamy charge, it probably did not matter.

'But what about the sentence that will be handed out?' I asked, only to be told that they did not think he would receive a very harsh sentence, as it was 'not really seen as a very serious crime, particularly when no distress has been caused'.

'No distress caused!' I said, aghast. 'He married me to defraud me of every penny I had, controlled me in fear for nearly six years and has also left me in over £56,000 of debt with three small children to support. If that is not counted as distress, what is?'

My outrage finally seemed to register, and the man on the other end of the line told me they would look into how my statement could be introduced into evidence.

On 3 September 2006, Will was still emailing me, trying to persuade me to meet him and telling me how much he loved me and wanted to find some way for us to get back together.

Although I was adamant that I would not see him, I also did not want to antagonise him, so just calmly kept saying no.

On 4 September, he was rearrested and once more charged with not registering his address. This time he was remanded in custody, and a fixed trial date was set for 23 November 2006.

Bolstered by the knowledge that Will was incarcerated, I did finally go to the police myself and report how Will had defrauded me; however, I was nervous about doing so as the taser was an illegal weapon and had been in my house. Will had told me to remain quiet about it because otherwise I would be charged with possession of it. At this point, however, I decided to face the music and come clean about everything. I did not want this hanging over me any more.

When I first called the station, the policeman I talked to clearly thought I was a nutter, and did nothing. When I called back and spoke to him again, he at least listened, and through the course of the conversation realised that I was serious. He even apologised for his earlier assumption and came out to see me immediately. He arrived within fifteen minutes and sat drinking glasses of water and regularly picking up his jaw off the floor. I asked him about the taser and whether I would be in trouble for having had it in my possession. He asked if I had brought it into the house and I said, 'No, Will had it delivered.' He asked if I had ever taken it out of the house. Once again I said no; Will had removed it when we moved out. He then said that basically it was not something to worry about, as it had been Will's possession.

He had never come across anything like this before. Although at first he did not think that any crime had been committed – lying to your wife to get money from her is not a criminal offence – he gradually started to realise the full extent of the situation. He wanted to involve the Scottish fraud squad and asked them if they could view Will marrying me as having been part of a plan to defraud me of my meagre money. The case proceeded, and another officer became involved. He had been a tax-fraud inspector for nineteen years and was used to looking through credit-card statements. He was very hopeful that we could get a conviction based on the fact that I had been asked to move around large sums of money. This would leave a trail – particularly because the bank keeps the slips that I'd had to sign when depositing the cash. That and the email evidence I held, which showed that the cash Will had asked for matched the amounts taken out of my bank account, would create a pretty good case. He presented his opinion to the Scottish fraud squad, but they said that because the money had not been put into his account but someone else's, there could be 'reasonable doubt' that he meant to defraud me, and therefore it would not stand up in a criminal court.

At this point, I gave up, as it was clear that they thought my case was too hard to nail down. However, they did say it would stand up in a civil court and I could pursue it that way – but what would be the point? I would just end up being another person that Will owed money to; he would only end up trying to get that money from another victim and I did not want to be responsible for that.

Eventually, in November 2006, one week before Will's trial, I was told that the CPS had decided that they would like a Victim Impact Statement from me. This is a statement that is submitted into evidence and allows a victim to elucidate the effect that the crime has had on him or her – particularly if the accused has indicated that they will plead guilty. Finally, I had the opportunity to have my say, and the judge would know what Will had done. I was glad, if exhausted.

I wrote the following and gave it to the Scottish policeman to send:

Victim Impact Statement – Mary Turner Thomson taken from Mary Turner Thomson who is JORDAN's second wife and currently lives in Edinburgh.

Prior to meeting Will Jordan, I was a single mother with a one-year-old baby daughter. I owned my own two-bedroom home overlooking the sea in Portobello, Edinburgh, which I had been paying a mortgage and endowment on for over ten years. I held a full-time job as a business adviser, trainer and marketing consultant, which paid me just under £30,000 per annum. I was a confident, happy and personally responsible individual who taught motivational courses for business people and schools alike. I believed that all people were basically good and I did not even know of the existence of psychopaths.

Will Jordan contacted me through an online dating site in November 2000. Shortly after our relationship started Will Jordan proved to me that he was a CIA intelligence officer based in the UK, specialising in the Palestinian/Israeli area (proof which I now know to be fabricated). He would often have to travel and was away from home for long periods. After initially telling me he was infertile, he left me from three months pregnant until our daughter was three months old (from July 2001–May 2002) and without funds, while also terrified for his life as he told me he was supposedly working in the massacre city of Jenin in the Palestinian territories. I now know that he was in fact only fifteen miles away living in Gullane with his other wife (with whom he had a new baby and four other children) and their nanny (with whom Will had apparently also had another new baby).

I married Will Jordan on 26 October 2002 at Victoria Street Registry Office, when our first child was eight months old. He told me he wanted out of the CIA and into a 'normal life'. However, he also told me that he needed funds to get him out. He started a business with me named as MD and worked as an IT contractor through it, moving the money he needed through the business. Will also asked me to get credit cards, which I did; he even applied for more cards for me. He told me that he had contacts with car-hire companies, cinemas and property agents which could move the money he needed for him. This would protect me by not having his name on anything. The credit cards all ran out in 2005 and the credit he used has left me with debts amounting to around £56,000. This leaves me still awaiting bankruptcy as I have to wait for one of the creditors to take me to court before I can declare bankruptcy in Scotland.

Will had me living in fear of kidnapping and torture by 'unsavouries' or other agents, and issued me with a taser (stun gun), training me how to use it. He brought it into the house and then took it away again over a year later when I had to move in with my parents in March 2005 – I believe this is the taser which was discovered in the Merc car he was driving (also in my name). I had to move in with my parents when I was pregnant by Will Jordan for the second time, as I did not even have enough money to feed my children.

Will Jordan manipulated me into selling my flat to raise £100,000, which he needed initially to buy his way out of the CIA; and then more and more money later to protect Will and my family from fabricated threats and dangerous 'unsavouries' who had discovered our whereabouts and who were using this information to blackmail money from him. All in all and including the credit cards, the total is just short of £200,000. When I had nothing left I was asked to raise more money and sold the endowment life-insurance policy which was the last thing I had left and the only thing I had retained for the children. Then I was encouraged to borrow money from my family, which I did as well – one instance of this was £2,000 borrowed from my brother to avoid 'dire consequences' on Xmas Eve 2004.

I was told about the charges against Will Jordan in January 2006 but Will convinced me that the other 'wife' was just an asset for the CIA and the fraud a mistake. He told me that the charge of 'not registering his address' pertained to an assignment he was given by the CIA – to get information out of a particularly nasty character in a sex-offenders' prison, and they set up a bogus sex charge to get him into the same prison. Will even arranged for me to talk to the 'victim' of that crime, who confirmed that Will Jordan was an intelligence officer and the crime fabricated (I now know that she was also under his control at that time). Will Jordan wrote a letter for me to send to the Crown Prosecution Service in March 2006, which I signed and faxed as told.

I only discovered the depth of Will Jordan's deception when his other wife rang me on 5 April 2006 and then came up to Edinburgh to talk to me. She proved to me that she was in fact a wife, not an 'asset' as he had told me, and that she had five children with Will. She showed me photographs of the children who bore a strong resemblance to my own children. It was only then that I saw through his lies to the truth and ended my relationship with Will Jordan. From April to September 2006 Will Jordan continued contact trying to pull me back into line with wild stories of how he was a victim in all this, saying 'history would vindicate him'. He continued asking me to take him back as my husband and only stopped when he was arrested again and held on remand in September 2006.

I have spent the past six months trying to recover from this and uncover the truth to find some peace, but what I have found is a trail of similar stories from other women – including his first wife in the USA who discovered three other women he had been having relationships with at the time; and had Will Jordan imprisoned in 1991 for defrauding her and leaving her with huge debts on his behalf after only one year of marriage. I believe that Will Jordan is a psychopath, which is 'a personality disorder characterised by deceit on a scale most of us cannot imagine. These people are not crazy; they know exactly what they are doing.' (Quoted from the www.love-fraud.com website.) Here is how Robert D. Hare,

Ph.D., begins his book about psychopaths Without Conscience:

'Psychopaths are social predators who charm, manipulate and ruthlessly plough their way through life, leaving a broad trail of broken hearts, shattered expectations and empty wallets. Completely lacking in conscience and feelings for others, they selfishly take what they want and do as they please, violating social norms and expectations without the slightest sense of guilt or regret.'

My life has been devastated by this, financially, emotionally and professionally. I am now a single mother with three children to support on my own – a seven-year-old girl, a four-year-old girl and one-year-old boy. The two older children are extremely distressed by the situation and have fallen behind in their school work, and the four-year-old regularly cries for her daddy, which breaks my heart and causes me to break down. I am particularly distressed for the children because I now know he conceived them simply to control and manipulate me – he has no emotional connection with them at all. I will have to provide them with additional support to counteract the damage that his actions have caused them now and in the future.

I am unable to work due to the stress of this situation, while I try to counteract the devastating realisation that I have been manipulated and conned from the very outset by the one person I loved and trusted for nearly six years; that he married me simply to defraud me of the money I had spent my life earning and working hard for. He has kept me in a state of stress for the past six years by keeping me

exhausted, in fear and in emotional/mental isolation
simply to control me as a game and support his other
family or families.

I am now on income support living in rented
accommodation and getting £57 per week to live on
and awaiting bankruptcy with the £56,000 debt
hanging over me. I am devoid of any capital assets
or any savings. My confidence and self-esteem are
shattered, and more particularly my ability to trust
others is completely gone. I believed Will loved me,
I believed that his work with the CIA was real and
the proof he showed me genuine; and I believed that
the money he needed was for our survival, but it
was simply a game to him to take everything from
me, and our children, to give to others. I also live
with the horror that he might have been grooming
my eldest daughter as he seems to target women who
already have children.

I cannot imagine that I will ever truly recover
from this, or ever trust anyone again.

Will's defence received the statement the day before his trial and he duly changed all pleas to 'guilty'. By then, however, Alice and I were both on our way, so we attended the trial anyway.

23

The Trial

On 22 November 2006, I travelled down to Oxford with my new sister-in-law — a lovely girl who has made my brother happy after he had his heart broken and suffered traumas of his own. She is a very compassionate person and I was so comforted by her presence and support; she listened to me talk non-stop all the way down, trapped less than two feet from me in a train seat with no means of escape. She was my minder and anchor for the whole three days.

In the run-up to the trial, I had become more and more anxious about seeing Will. I had not seen him since January, when he had been my gentle and romantic husband. Everything that I had found out about him since was in complete contrast to the man I knew, to the man I had thought existed. I spent a long time working out what I was going to wear and thinking about things that I did have control over, because I knew I would not have control over anything else.

Without the children around me or the distractions of the daily grind, the train journey made me focus on what I had previously tried to avoid. Everything was very vivid and clear. Ideas and thoughts flooded back, along with a tidal wave of memories: of how loving he had been and how his face had lit up when he walked through our door; of nights I had wandered around the house having heard a noise, feeling too frightened to go to sleep; of conversations in restaurants conducted on napkins; and the pieces of the puzzle as I had discovered them over recent months. I was full of terror about what he would do. Would he look at me with love and fill me with doubts about whether or not he had cared at all? Would he look at me with hate for being there? Or would he glance at me with disdain, or not look at me at all? My doctor told me not to look at his face but only at his shoulders. I had to protect myself from getting hooked into his world again and take control back for myself. However, I knew I would have to look into those eyes. I knew they would tell me something – and they did.

That evening, we met up with Alice. We had become firm friends under very strange circumstances and it was very good to finally put a face to the voice; I felt a warm affection for this woman who had started this whole process and released me.

When we went back to the hotel, I found it almost impossible to get to sleep, and when I did manage to drift off I had terrible nightmares. Eventually I gave up and found myself lying awake just waiting for the morning to come. I wanted time to rush forward and everything to be over.

I was up and dressed early. We joined Alice before all heading off to the court feeling very anxious. When we arrived, we met up with others – my aunt and cousin; Peter, the police officer who had worked solely on Will's case for the past year; Malcolm, the businessman whom Will had conned, and so on.

Alice and I were called into a witness room by a representative of the CPS, who told us what to expect and how the trial would proceed. That is when I started to shake. There was a bit more of a wait and then we were called in. My shaking got worse and I tried to control my breathing. I realised that I was shaking from pure fear; I was terrified of seeing him – terrified of the idea that he might still be able to control me.

We walked into the court together and Alice and I sat side by side. Directly behind us sat a young woman, and I realised who she was almost immediately – it was Anna, whom Will had molested as a child, come to witness his decline. I did not acknowledge her but just sat down.

Will was brought in and Alice held my arm, even now looking after me. He was dressed in a T-shirt and trousers, looking less groomed than I had ever seen him before – almost like he couldn't be bothered. He stood, scanning to see who was there, and although I had been told not to look at him, I had to; I had to know what his eyes would tell me. The man standing there stared in our direction. He was empty, completely blank. He stared at all three of us – Alice, Anna and me. Cold. Unemotional. Blank. It was an empty, hard stare that lasted an eternity but with nothing behind it. I simply stared back, doing my best to stay equally blank. Then he turned to face the judge as he entered.

Throughout the trial, it was like watching someone getting a parking ticket. He showed no emotion; the man sitting in the dock bore no resemblance to the man I had married. Was this the true Will Jordan – a blank sheet, a dark mirror that had simply reflected my own desires and wants? Was that how he succeeded so well with so many women? It did not matter. The man I had loved did not exist.

The judge was clearly very aware of Will's character as he heard the charges and asked questions. Particularly, he asked, 'Does Mr Jordan have the right to remain in this country?'

His barrister actually sounded embarrassed when he said, 'Yes, your honour, by dint of his being married to a British national.'

'Hmm,' the judge said. 'Do you have the right to work in this country, Mr Jordan?'

'Yes, sir,' Will said calmly.

The judge looked down at his papers. 'Pity!' he said, loudly enough for the whole court to hear.

I felt that this man had Will's measure and I was reassured.

As Will had changed his plea to guilty, the case only lasted twenty minutes. Thanks to the prosecution barrister, the judge knew that both Alice and I were in the court and spoke to us directly. He said, 'I want both Alice Kean and Mary Turner Thomson to know that I have read and understood their Victim Impact Statements and I understand the distress, sadness and trauma they have both had to endure at the hands of this man. As far as is feasibly possible, this will be reflected in the sentence he will receive.'

Then turning back to Will, he said, 'And it will be a custodial sentence, Mr Jordan, you understand that?'

'Yes, sir,' Will said, still relaxed.

I do not remember Will leaving the court, though I know I stood up as the judge left. Apparently I remained standing as Will was led out, continuing to shake throughout. I remember a determination to hold on in front of Will, to remain solid and strong. But after he was gone, I collapsed into the seat and wept long and hard. I was not conscious or aware of where I was, only of a great sorrow, a heavy and hard burden finally coming to the surface. It was over. I cried for the years of pain, and for my kids who would never have a father; for the man I loved who'd never existed and for myself for being so abused and taken in. I cried and Alice held me while I wept.

When I came round from my grief, it was gone; it had finally come to the surface, been experienced and dissipated. I was free and could finally move forward; I could face a new future without this past holding me back.

Sentencing was deferred for twenty-eight days for reports by the probation department, including possible medical reports. I was told by the CPS that the judge wrote a note on the file stating that the most senior medical representative was to interview him and absolutely not to be taken in, as the man was extremely manipulative.

So we went home.

The media coverage came next, and finally the story was made public. The hardest part was over, and although there was still a long way to go I felt I was turning a corner and getting back on track.

I got satisfaction from the trial not because the man who stood there bore no resemblance to the man I had married, but because of what the judge had said. Somehow his words meant everything; having the vindication that what this man had done to me was wrong helped beyond measure.

24

RECOVERY

I did tell my family, bit by bit. In the first few days after I had met Michelle, I told them that I had left Will, then that it had all been lies – his job, our life. Over time, I told them about the debt he'd left me in; then about his other wife, other women and the other children; finally and later I told them that he was a convicted paedophile. That was and still is the hardest part for me. Gradually, as I told them, and as I talked to people, I started to get my brain back, started to see more clearly and understand what had happened to me.

Up until June 2006, Will constantly told me he still wanted to support the kids and me, and that as long as he could still work at least he would be able to provide for us. He begged me not to ruin this for 'us'. He told me that there was more work; that the company he had been contracted to were happy with him, and that his boss Christopher had offered him several lucrative private contracts. But I knew that this was not the case, because I was now talking to Christopher myself. Will had disappeared from their company and not returned his pass or his laptop; neither had he submitted his final month's timesheet – worth around £6,000. Will kept telling me that he was there, that he was talking to Christopher, but I would be on the other phone to Chris, who thought that Will was having a nervous breakdown.

Will kept trying to lure me back to him, trying to suck me in, but I now knew how he worked: distraction, evasion, promises to answer a question but never actually doing so, declarations of love, promises of a better life and support for the children, threats and attempts to generate pity, then anger and betrayal. The trick was to keep the victim talking, to keep the lines of communication open, to find a weakness and exploit it. He had to tug at my heartstrings and make me feel guilty or responsible – make me feel bad about myself and my need to be loved. He seemed sure that eventually something would work.

However, now free of the hypnotic hold he had over me, I refused to let myself be distracted from the point or the questions to which I wanted answers, and kept bringing him back to them. Armed with information and the confidence I had been given by his other victims, I could now see what he was doing and, though I could feel the pressure to bend to his will, I did not yield.

I offered to talk to him, to be someone to whom he could tell the whole truth. I wanted answers, and in an attempt to draw him out I suggested that it might help him to get the story off his chest. He said he appreciated this but kept repeating that he would have to wait until after the trial before he could explain everything that had happened. He said that he knew what I now thought of him and, though he completely understood where it came from and why I might think this way, it was disappointing to him and it hurt that I could have spent so much time with him and say I loved him, yet really believe even half the nonsense that he had heard spouted.

I told him that if he did not tell me the truth I would have to work it out for myself, though I did not tell him how much I had already uncovered. He said: 'If you haven't already done so, tickle your resource pool . . . nobody will tell you anything more about me than you think you already know . . . the answers and explanations you want are not floating out there somewhere . . . no other wives, no more kids, nothing of that nature . . . If it was so straightforward it would already be there, so please don't tell me about finding out for yourself.'

Will said that the policeman involved in the case was only going on what his computer system told him; that the police had a marriage certificate that had been created to hide the truth of the situation and a police record that was fabricated. According to him, Michelle had her own motivations, but he wouldn't explain what he meant by this; he stated that I knew nothing about Devi or I would not even bring that up, and even claimed that Alexis simply did not exist, implying that she was a character made up by the CIA.

When I asked him about his other children by the other women, the nanny and Devi, he said: 'Insofar as there are others, I have honoured my responsibilities.' But when I queried what he meant by that and asked if this was where my money had gone, he denied it. He just repeated that he had honoured his responsibilities and would say no more about it.

He kept assuring me that he was still working and intended to support the children we had together, but I knew this was a lie.

We went over and over the same ground. When I continued to question him, he affected hurt, though he admitted to lies he had told – including having sex with other women and fathering other children. He would get angry, tired and upset but it would always come back to thinly disguised attempts to draw me back into his fabricated world. He would come up with great lines like, 'Don't wax hypocritical on me, Mary . . . the fact that I lied about a million things was no secret . . . but what you lost sight of and you let go of was the fact that underneath anything I ever said for other reasons, I always, always loved you and you know I did . . . you felt that connection.' He ranted that he knew more than I could ever begin to understand about sacrifice. I was supposed to be his wife but I had given up on him. I had run out and closed the door without even a 'by your leave', and worst of all I would not even talk to him face to face.

In the end, unable to get control of me again, he would finish each conversation by saying that I was 'mean' or that he was just too tired to continue and would talk to me the next day. He would sign off with a promise to tell me something more to make sure that I kept communicating with him.

He only gave up contacting me and trying to get me to meet him when he was arrested in September 2006 and put into jail awaiting trial on 23 November. He even used my mother's illness as a way of trying to get back in – asking me repeatedly if he could be there to hold my hand and console me, to say goodbye to her himself. He tried anything he could think of to get me to agree to meet him face to face, because if I did, half the battle would be won – he would have a way back in.

Back in June 2006, I contacted the social worker – Brenda – and asked her to visit my home, to tell her the story. I explained how I had been duped into believing Will and how I now knew it had all been lies. She listened carefully and was obviously relieved. She understood what had happened and why I had reacted the way I did. She was sympathetic and helpful, and glad to hear he would never be allowed back.

Brenda asked to meet my eldest daughter, Will's stepdaughter, which I arranged, and Robyn came through. As always, Robyn was bubbly, full of energy and showing off in front of a guest. She bounced in and jumped into my lap, every bit the normal, happy and lively seven-year-old that she was.

Brenda chatted with her for a few minutes, I do not even remember what about. Afterwards, Robyn went back to her game and I looked at Brenda.

'You are right. She certainly shows no signs of having been molested,' she said. 'Paedophiles tend to stay within their own preferred age range, and as he molested a girl who was nine until she was thirteen, Robyn is probably too young. You will never know if he had anything planned.'

I felt cold. This was the hardest part to deal with: I had lived with and loved someone who had molested a child. I broke down in tears.

'You are a good mother, Mary,' Brenda said. 'I can see that you are a very good mother, you love your children and you will get through this.'

I still don't believe that Will is a sexual predator of children. Nor do I think he was grooming my eldest daughter. I think he is a psychopath and that he molested Anna as a means of alienating her from her mother, thereby ensuring the mother had no one to talk to. He was trying to see how far he could push the boundaries and still get away with it.

I think that he ran out of other excitements, and psychopaths need excitement; they need to keep pushing the boundaries, keep controlling, keep manipulating – even when caught.

As clarity came back into my life, I took certain important steps. I had told my mother everything, because there was not a lot of time. My lovely mother – who had been there for me always; who had seen me through everything; who had been my children's surrogate parent because of the absence of their father, and who now was the only person I truly knew loved me unconditionally – was dying. She was undergoing treatment for cancer and I needed her to cut me out of her will, which she did. I had got myself into this mess and I did not want her hard-earned life savings paying off the debt he had left me with. I would rather not inherit anything from my parents than have them pay for my mistakes. This was my responsibility and, as the credit-card companies persistently point out, I gave him permission to use the cards and therefore the debts were mine.

My mother wondered if he had drugged me. She could not fathom how he had managed to manipulate me into believing so much. It's possible, but I think that he just kept me exhausted and malleable. Any new mother who is sleep-deprived will tell you how hard it is to rationalise when constantly exhausted. He had me living in fear and I was dependent on him. He would have me sit up late at night talking on MSN and call me or text me in the wee hours. He kept me stressed, which is a state of depression in itself, and he had me live in silence and emotional isolation so that I could not ask for help.

I had worked as a marketing consultant and trainer, but since my world had crumbled it was difficult to focus or think about anything else. I could not work, and signed on. I spent time with my mother, trying to make her last few months as comfortable as possible. I watched her fight and struggle to breathe, never giving up, always defying the prognosis. Until the last day, the night before she died, when she finally did not want to carry on. She told me, 'This is not much fun.' As I said goodnight to her I knew I was probably saying goodbye. I actually hoped I was saying goodbye, because I knew that was what she wanted. I miss her every day.

Mum was so good at practical advice, so solidly rational. More than anything she was glad that my nightmare was over and I was free to start again. She admitted to me that she had worried how I would manage to divorce him when the time came – as she knew it eventually would. She was glad that as my marriage was bigamous, I would not have to do that. I would have to get my marriage voided, but with his conviction in hand that would not be difficult.

My mother had an amazing life herself and always wanted to write her story down. She had started but never finished it. So she told me to write mine – for me, for my children, for his other victims, and for everyone who could learn from it. Right up to the end she was thinking of us and trying to help us face the future.

My mum died on 15 August 2006. Two days later, I went to writing workshops at the Edinburgh Book Festival and started to write down what had happened – this story. I started to write it as I had experienced it at the time – the lies as I was told then, and the truth as it was revealed to me. I still believe there will be others out there – other women and, more than likely, other children, still trapped and still silent. What is the truth? I don't think I will ever know the full extent of it, but the more I find out, the deeper this goes, the more I realise that he was not just a 'liar'.

I started to research psychopaths and to understand what they are and do. I found sites that were invaluable to me, such as www.lovefraud.com. It was amazingly helpful, because it lists others who have been through almost exactly the same experience. I was able to read about other intelligent women, and a few men, who had been used and manipulated, left broken-hearted and bankrupt, their life earnings and everything they possessed gone. What amazed me more than anything, however, was that I could not find one book written by the wife of a bigamist or victim of a psychopath. I suppose the shame of being conned is too strong. It is hard to stand up and wave at people saying, 'This happened to me, I was manipulated', but I feel a strong compulsion to do it for everyone who has gone through the same pain.

I had not known before this happened to me that there were people out there like Will, and yet it is estimated that 1 per cent of the population are psychopaths – ranging from sleazebags to serial killers. It is not a mental illness or a curable psychological condition. It is a personality disorder – incurable and untreatable.

They have no emotion, no moral code and no empathy for others. Psychopaths are predators and see everyone else as prey, although even they themselves do not necessarily recognise this.

As someone that is empathic, I often intuitively know what other people are feeling. I thought that I was a good judge of character, but Will took me in completely – maybe because I could not sense his emotions; maybe because he did not have any. I may never know.

25

The Future

In May 2006, I recovered sufficiently from the shock to start pulling my life together. I went to the doctor's and sat waiting to see someone. I knew I would have to put the story to them succinctly and answer questions, but I also knew the story itself sounded stranger than fiction. As luck would have it, I saw a student doctor on the last day of her training. I am amazed she didn't think it was a practical joke! She interviewed me and took notes. Then she had to get the qualified doctor, now my ongoing doctor, to see me.

When he came in, she relayed the story. 'Mary has just discovered she has been in a bigamist relationship with a conman and convicted paedophile who convinced her he was a CIA intelligence officer and has ripped her off of everything she owned, leaving her on the verge of bankruptcy with three small children to support.'

I was impressed with her concise analysis of the situation, but I will never forget his calmly phrased, matter-of-fact reply. Without even the raise of an eyebrow, he said, 'That's all a very sad story, but what is the medical issue here?'

She was stumped for a moment, and I laughed out loud before saying, 'I need a medical certificate for the DSS.'

He gave me some advice about writing the story down and setting goals, all of which I already knew, and in fact had taught as part of training courses in personal responsibility and motivation. Then he gave me a medical certificate stating I was unfit to work due to 'stress', under the heading of 'marital problems', and I left, wishing the student doctor well in her future career.

My doctor has proved brilliant and has seen me regularly. He told me that although I initially thought the stress was caused by my world crumbling, the truth is I had been suffering with stress for the past six years and that Will was keeping me that way to control me. He took a single mother with a small child, who was therefore already dealing with sleeplessness and under stress, and continued to develop that stress, adding the fear and isolation in a controlled way as he went. It helped enormously to have a no-nonsense medical practitioner state that it could have happened to anyone.

There have been quite a few laughs through the recovery process, and a lot of funny stories – not least on the day that Michelle and I met. We went into a cafe and up to the counter, talking all the way. The chap behind the counter said, 'Can I help you?'

We both looked at him and I said, 'I don't know. We've just found out that we are married to the same man.' I had a compulsion to say it out loud, to anyone, to articulate it and know that it was real.

He looked stunned for a moment and was left speechless.

'OK, well, just two cups of tea, then,' I said.

Then he said, 'You want to share a pot?'

We both saw the funny side and laughed together.

At other times, it was people's reactions that made me laugh. I called a friend I had not talked to in a long time and asked her how she was. She told me at length about the last six months and how awful they had been. She had broken her heel bone and been unable to work; her husband had to carry her up and down the stairs while she had been housebound for months. She was ranting about how difficult and unpleasant it had been, and I listened, very glad to be talking about something other than myself. After about forty minutes, she ran out of steam and asked me how I was, to which I replied, 'No, you really don't want to know!'

She pushed me for an answer and I eventually said, 'I'll take your broken heel and raise you bigamy, fraud, firearms and paedophilia.'

Like most of my friends, she was great. She was supportive and kind; she knew me well enough not to offer simpering sympathy, and knew I was strong enough to weather the storm. I enjoyed making her laugh about the situation and felt that it had made her feel a bit better about her own.

I would crack jokes to people to break the tension when I told them the story. They would say I was looking good having lost so much weight, and I would say, 'It's the bigamy diet – bigamy, little of me!' I think it helped other people come to terms with it, as it affected everyone around me, particularly those who had met and known him.

But I couldn't smile through it all, particularly the sinister side effects I realised his behaviour had caused. My memory of events was at times skewed, and as I tried to mull over everything that had happened, I discovered that I had various false memories. For example, I seemed to remember having talked to Michelle in the past, and felt sure that I'd had firm proof that she was his 'asset'. I even remembered discussing with Will how I had talked to her directly. But when I tried to pin down that memory and work out when it had happened, I couldn't – the only clear memory was of him telling me I had spoken to her. As clarity came back, I realised how he had done this. He had been on the phone to Michelle in front of me, arranging for me to speak to her, but it was not immediately convenient; we would have to call back in a few minutes because she had a report to finish. What he would then do in instances like this was distract me by dropping a cup of coffee, getting a call to depart or just continuing to top up my glass of wine and then seducing me. The next day he would talk as if the event had happened, and gradually the memory of what he told me would settle into my mind rather than what had actually occurred.

Gradually I came to recognise that a lot of the things I had believed so totally – his work, his travelling, his enemies, his achievements, things that I accepted as facts – were actually just things that I had been *told* were facts.

It became clear that I had not talked to Michelle before 5 April 2006. These false memories were all revealed when I started to write things down, because I had to put them in perspective. The further I moved away from him, the more I understood what had happened and the control he'd had, even over my thoughts. The control weakened when he was away from me, though, and reality came back into focus – just as the certainties of a dream fade when you wake up.

I was deeply disturbed by this phenomenon and wanted to know more about it. I even researched it online and discovered a training course on 'black ops hypnosis', which teaches conversational manipulative hypnosis – using negative psychology to control whoever you want. I bought the package and studied it, not so that I could learn to do it, but just so I could understand it and avoid it happening to me again. It was fascinating, as Will had used every technique on me – every single one. Not any more, though – now I could see how it worked, I would not be influenced again. Now I knew what he was.

I realised that we do take most things at face value: when people tell us they work in a certain company, we do not call the company to check. When did you last ask your doctor to show you his medical qualifications or ask a taxi driver to show you his driving licence? We just assume that these people are qualified to do the jobs they do. We do not automatically expect people to lie to us, and if they have proof to back themselves up, we trust them and expect them to continue telling us the truth.

There will always be a lot of unanswered questions. Where did the money go and what was it used for? How and why did he have no hair on his chest when we met, and how did it start to grow? There was no stubble from shaving or waxing, and I saw the individual hairs appear. It was a physical signal of his infertility and his proof that he had grown out of it over the years. Yet Michelle said that he had always had a hairy chest. That still does not make sense to me and although I have asked many people, no one has managed to explain it. Will often used it as an example of physical proof. Other questions that remain include how he knew that Yasser Arafat was not dead, and how he had access to the videotapes of executions prior to them being aired on television. Also, who were the people that I spoke to, believing they were his parents, and how did he get them to talk and lie to me?

I think the only reason I will ever find as to why he does this – and has done to so many people – is that it is just the way he is wired. I have to accept what he is and that this is the way he lives his life – but I do not have to accept him or anyone like him in *my* life.

Twenty-eight days after the trial I travelled down overnight on my own to witness the sentencing. This time, I did not need support or help. I knew that it would just be me and Peter, the policeman, and I was OK with that. It was the final chapter and I wanted to see it through to the end.

I sat in the corridor outside the court, waiting. I had arrived early and was looking around me. I heard the hushed voices of anxious people, watched the witnesses, the stenographers and the barristers in black swirling robes and white cravats moving up and down the corridor with armfuls of papers.

I felt calm in comparison to how I'd felt at the trial, when I had been so scared of facing him and seeing his disdain. Now I was eager for closure, completion. I was ready to start my new life and leave all this behind me.

Peter arrived and said hello, indicating my identity to the others waiting in the hallway. One by one they talked to me, the press-agency staff and the STV reporters. I told them that I couldn't comment as I was writing a book, but we all chatted in general about the case. I agreed to give them a passing comment and photo on the way out.

Then we were called in. The sentencing proved to be a more informative affair than the trial, and took over two hours. There was a new judge. First, the three indictments were read out in full. The first indictment listed two counts of failing to register his address under the Sexual Offences Act. The second indictment had six counts – five of fraud pertaining to his use of Alice's credit card and defrauding her of money, and one count of bigamy. The third indictment contained one count of possession of a prohibited weapon. There was also a committal for sentence regarding another charge of not registering his address.

The judge said he had read the Victim Impact Statements and made it clear that he could not take the additional debts I had mentioned in my statement into account. The prosecution barrister pointed out that it was simply to put the crimes into context.

Will's previous convictions in the US and the UK were raised, along with the issue of compensation, though it was doubted by all that Will had any assets at all with which to compensate those he had defrauded.

The judge asked what the maximum sentences were for the crimes, and was told that for not registering his address, it was five years; for obtaining property by deception, ten years; for invasion of liability – the failed attempted use of another's credit card – five years; for bigamy, seven years; for possession of firearms, ten years.

He also looked at previous convictions that had set a precedent for bigamy cases. They could only find three cases since 1978 that had resulted in a custodial sentence – the maximum being eighteen months. The judge said that none of these cases was helpful, because this was by far the worst he had ever come across. He said, 'Nothing comes close to this.'

The defence stepped up and stated that Will's reason for not registering his address – which he was obliged to do as a registered sex offender under the Sexual Offences Act – was because he thought that this was only necessary for seven years, not ten, and until 2004 he was registered in Lancashire.

I wanted to scream, 'LIAR,' as he was living in Gullane in 2000 and, as I understand it, was actually charged with not registering his address there. His defence also stated that the taser was bought on eBay for his own defence.

The medical report stated that there was a low-to-medium risk that Will would reoffend, and the judge said with heavy sarcasm, 'I'm not sure I agree with that!'

He queried why a psychiatric report had not been requested, and was told this was because Will was not deemed 'dangerous'. Also, the defence said that bigamy should only result in a custodial sentence if the victim had suffered some injury in consequence.

Again, the judge simply said, 'A prison sentence must happen here.' He recognised that injury does not necessarily have to be physical.

The court adjourned for fifteen minutes to allow him to consider and review, and we left to get some fresh air and take a break.

As we got up to leave, I was approached by another woman, elegant and clearly well educated, who spoke to me only briefly. This was Helen, the woman whom Will had abandoned while she was heavily pregnant: another of his victims. The media coverage had alerted her to Will's whereabouts, so she had come to see him sentenced. She furtively gave me her phone number, pressed into my hand on a scrap of paper. 'Call me tomorrow,' she said.

For Helen, finding out where he was after he abandoned her has, in her own words, provided her with some sense of closure. Not final closure, obviously, as she still has a child who has no knowledge of their father. But at least having an awareness of who he really is could, in the fullness of time, help her child understand their paternal origin.

There were surely still others out there: more women, and more children . . .

For me, the discussions with Helen about her experience with Will confirmed that I was right to go public. Following a newspaper article written about me, some online media contributors said that I was humiliating myself by standing up to be counted as a victim. But by bringing this out into the open, I felt that I was making both past and potential future victims aware of this man and, hopefully, protecting them.

When we reconvened, the judge spoke.

> *Mr Jordan, you are forty-one, a conman, a convicted paedophile, a bigamist and an inveterate exploiter of vulnerable women. You have little or no regard for their feelings despite a belated expression of remorse. You have caused significant emotional damage to*

three women and financial loss to certainly one – Alice Kean.

I have read the Victim Impact Statements of Alice Kean and your bigamist wife Mary Turner Thomson, who is present in the court. You are to be sentenced regarding the deception of Alice Kean for wrongful use of her credit card and also two separate charges of not registering your address. It is clear that you pay little regard for that legal nicety.

In addition, a taser was found in the car, a car that you couldn't afford without cheating others.

You pleaded not guilty on 7 July 2006 to counts one to five, all deception offences, but guilty of bigamy. You also pleaded guilty to possession of a prohibited weapon and to one of two counts of not registering your address under the Sexual Offences Act.

On counts one to five, although you did notify change of plea, this was too late and you only get a ten per cent discount for that.

The position, put shortly, is that you obtained the trust and love of Alice Kean, and took £4,500 off her by deception by making various false assurances regarding paying her back and that you wanted to marry her. You abused her credit card, which is counts two to five. The stun gun deserves no further comment. Sex-offender offences show that you do not care about keeping the authorities informed. I do not accept that you did not know the length of time you had to register for.

I make it clear that I have read and taken into account all the papers, prosecution and Victim Impact Statements which demonstrate women *emotionally broken. The path to recovery for both women will be a difficult one.*

Regarding the pre-sentence report stating the likelihood of reoffending as being "low to medium", I simply do not agree with it. Looking at the facility of dishonesty, I find it hard to believe that the risk of reoffending is . . . "low".

For the counts of fraud I give twenty-one months. For the bigamy, none of the previous cases were of particular assistance apart from an immediate custodial sentence. This bigamy is a serious one and the effect is substantial, requiring being properly sentenced. Therefore I award it twenty-one months, making forty-one months so far.

For the taser, the sentence is nine months, making fifty-one months' running total. For the two counts of not registering his address, I think that it is of the utmost importance and of great public concern that the authorities are kept informed. I therefore give three months and six months, making nine months consecutive, bringing the total sentence to sixty months, or five years. Credit will be awarded for the one hundred and five days already served on remand.

◆ ◆ ◆

Five years – it was a good amount of time. It meant he'd be behind bars for two and a half years and bound over for the rest. It meant I was free and secure for at least two years and could now focus on my life, my children and my future. It was more than I had hoped for, though indeed I had not hoped for anything at all. It was justice: it was a sentence that said that what he had done to me and others was wrong.

Throughout the sentencing, I had not looked at Will. I avoided his eyes and looked past him, taking notes and absorbing what was happening. I was aware that he'd tried to catch my eye throughout, but I had resisted. Now I looked at him. The door was opened and he started to go through. Someone asked the barrister a question and he stopped, turning to look at them, then suddenly caught my gaze. He reacted instantly, giving a reflexive smile for a fraction of a second before he regained control and emptied his expression again. I remained blank and looked away.

26

Once Bitten . . .

When I look back over those six years, the questions that keep going round and round in my head are: 'How could you let this happen? Are you stupid?' And the answer, I guess, is yes, I suppose I was.

I have been deceived, duped and conned. I believed someone loved me and I believed that he was telling me the truth; just as I believe my doctor when he tells me the pills he prescribes are for my health, or my financial adviser when he tells me that I must pay a certain tax. I am gullible and trusting. I believed, and perhaps that makes me 'stupid' – but I am not alone.

Until shockingly late in the twentieth century, if a woman was raped she was often told that she had been 'asking for it' and that she was a 'loose woman'. The victims of this horrible crime were made to feel that it was their fault, and kept it a secret so that no one would know of their shame. There are still those today who do not report rape because of the humiliation and embarrassment, particularly in the case of date rape; there is often an attitude that they must have been 'stupid' to have trusted the person enough to go on a date with him – yet everyone goes out on dates! This attitude is wrong, and society as a whole knows it is wrong.

It wasn't until the 1970s that people really started to talk openly about being molested or abused as children. Today, in contrast, there are numerous books about this very subject, because society is starting to change its attitude and say that such victims should not have to be ashamed of what happened to them. Why, then, should I be ashamed of what happened to me? What Will Jordan put me and these other women through is abuse – abuse of trust and of love; abuse and manipulation of power. Not only that, he is also guilty of fraud and theft through deception. Yes, I a grown woman and not a child, but he manipulated me as if I were a child, trapping me in silence and stress, in a world with which I was unfamiliar and which I was uninformed about. On top of losing everything and facing a future raising three children on my own, it is hard to know that society as a whole views me as some kind of fool.

I can understand this attitude, as in the past when I have read in the newspapers about bigamists' wives or victims of psychopaths, I have thought exactly the same: that they must be sad and really gullible to have been so easily manipulated – but I was wrong. It is not as clear-cut as that, and it is also not particularly easy to manipulate someone – it takes great skill and a very particular type of mind to do it.

The reaction of others to my story is always fascinating. Jaws drop and people are floored. Often I am asked with incredulity, 'And you believed him?' This is not said nastily but simply reflects their astonishment, as those who know me know that I am not a gullible 'daft lassie' or anybody's fool. I am a strong and confident woman and it stuns those who did not meet him because they know I am not stupid. Those who did know him were all taken in as well, to some degree.

Will was, and is, very good at what he does. He finds a victim, then finds a weakness and uses it. What is more, he has been doing it all his life and is very practised. I made it easy for him because I am a good person, because I have morals and stick by rules. I like to help people and, because I care, I was expertly guided into a position where I would have had to go against my nature and put people I cared about at risk if I did not follow the path laid out for me.

I was the perfect prey – a single mum who was a bit lonely and wanted someone to love me, someone to make me feel special. I wanted to be shown a little attention and be reminded that I was still a desirable woman and not just a mother – not so extraordinary, really. He kept me pregnant, sleep-deprived and silent, so I could never work through in my own head what was happening or articulate to others around me the insanity in which I was living. He always gave me hope that the situation was just about to change for the better.

I lived in fear, but fear is not something I have ever let control me. It was my ability to live with it, even though uncomfortable, that made it possible for him to continue – even my strength became my weakness, and trapped me. If I had been too dominated by the fear, I would have run away screaming from him and the situation.

I do not think he did it for the money, as I just did not have enough to make all his efforts worthwhile. I think the money was a measure of the control he had over me, a benchmark. When others had no money, he used sex: maybe that was where he would have taken me next.

Looking back, what I now see is a game of cat and mouse: the cat has no emotion or compassion for the mouse; it is about control. It is fun. Will is the predator; we are the prey. I do not take it personally, because it is not personal. The cat does not choose one mouse in particular; it could be any mouse that strays into its path.

It has taken me a long time to understand the extent of what Will has done to me and to others. It will take a longer time to come to terms with it fully and to pay off all the debts that he accrued in my name. But now, to me, this story is simply another part of my life. I have lived this, come through it and survived. Life is simpler than it has been over the past few years, and at the very least I do not have to live in fear any more. I am better off now with income support, because I am not giving every penny to him. I have money to feed my children and am used to living on a budget. Yes, I am in debt, his debt, but I will manage that somehow.

I am OK and not a gibbering wreck, because I am an intelligent and responsible adult, and because I have three children who depend on me and need me to be stronger than that.

I wake up in the morning and have a cup of coffee, play with my children and enjoy the peace. No longer do I rush to the computer to see if Will is online, or keep my mobile phone with me turned up loud just in case he calls. I am not constantly frustrated at being ignored and belittled by coming second to whatever he is doing, and I am finding more pleasure in the simple things in life. Possessions are not important; neither are money or clothes, or even a social life. I have lost everything I worked my whole adult life for, but I have what is most important – my children. People often say that they would give everything up for their children, but I have had the opportunity to prove that. My pleasure is in my children; my joy is seeing them grow up.

There were good times in the six years I was with Will, times of pure joy and wonder, but there were also times of disappointment, of total fear and desperation. Life has been dramatic and challenging, and I find the peaceful life of an ordinary soul very calming. I have not been destroyed by this experience; I have grown stronger and gained a better concept of what matters. My life has not been ruined; I simply lived for nearly six extraordinary years with some-one whom I now do not recognise.

I truly believe that we teach children by example, and when life throws a disaster at me, I sit my children down and talk to them, tell them the truth as best I can and tell them that we will be OK because we love one another. Whenever I am not sure what to do, how to cope, or how to work through something, I ask myself what advice I would give my children. I then try to live that advice, so they can see what I mean in practice.

So I have an opportunity to teach my children now. I have the chance to show them that you do not need to be bitter or hold on to sadness; that you can survive any situation and thrive by standing on the rock that is your own personal sense of self and responsibility. I can teach them that there is a moral code that will provide them with self-respect, and that although being honest and true may not earn them financial wealth, it will provide them with greater riches and a more beautiful life through the love and loyalty that it earns.

If this had happened to one of my children, I would have advised them to pull themselves up, breathe in and out until they were ready to move on, look after and find joy in their children, keep themselves healthy, get plenty of sleep, keep a diary and write it all down. I would have advised them to treasure the memories, good and bad, to learn from them and use them in a positive way. All memory is a learning experience and worthwhile regardless of its pain or joy. Pain is part of living and I am glad that I have lived, glad that I have my three wonderful children.

The kids are strong and know now that Will was married to someone else. They know he lied and I have told them it is my deci-sion that he won't be coming back, because we deserve better than to be lied to. I have also told them that he went to prison, because what he did was a crime. I explained to them that when they made bad decisions, like hitting each other, I made them sit on their beds and think about what they'd done. I explained that when you grow up, you are supposed to know right from wrong; if an adult makes a bad decision, they go to a court and a judge decides if they need time to think about their actions. In some cases the judge can then put them in jail if they've done wrong, or hurt someone.

I did eventually tell them that Will was convicted of molesting a child. It was the hardest thing to face, but they had to know. I have not, and never will, lie to them, ever. Children deserve the truth; they deserve to be included and not shut out or protected from reality.

I loved Will deeply – the man that I thought I knew, the absent father and the considerate lover – but he was just a mirror reflecting what I had wanted, a fictional character made up to control me. I do not believe, and never have believed, that anyone is 'evil'; I think that we are a combination of our nature and our experiences. There is a reason why Will does what he does – and that makes me feel sorry for him rather than bitter or angry. I don't think he will ever find happiness or satisfaction in simple joy; he will never be settled or have a normal life. I have to ensure that his children, my children, have a better chance at life and the hope of a brighter future. One thing I am sure of is that I will encourage them to live their dreams and do whatever they want, but to do it with positive respect for others, with honesty, integrity and truth.

Epilogue

A Word Of Warning

Dear reader,

I wanted to put something down as a word of advice and caution.

When I originally wrote *The Bigamist*, I thought Will Jordan was a sociopath and so used that term in the first two editions. However, the definitions have changed slightly in the last fifteen years and I would now describe him as a psychopath. The current definitions state that psychopathy is a result of nature (i.e. psychopaths are born that way) and sociopathy is a result of nurture (i.e. sociopaths are a product of their environment). But by adulthood the two are indistinguishable and therefore I now use the term 'psychopath' to cover both.

If you are thinking of, or are already involved in, online dating, please take my story as a cautionary tale. Although not everyone on dating sites is a psychopath or con artist, it is a wonderfully convenient facility for the worst of people to target their victims. I got caught because I didn't know people like this actually existed. BE AWARE. There are obvious signs that friends and family can see, but to which we can be blinded because we're too close. Check out anyone that you are dating: call their office, talk to their friends . . .

MEET their family and corroborate everything they tell you. You will know pretty quickly if their story holds up by talking openly to others. I did not do this enough, and allowed myself to be conned.

In the UK there are sites like www.192.com, which allow you to check out where someone lives and also who on the electoral roll lives with them. This can highlight whether someone is already married, but it does not always work (as in Will's case, as he didn't register his name anywhere). If someone is a director of a company, you can check that out through www.192.com as well, or alternatively you can use www.companieshouse.gov.uk.

Arm yourself with information and, more specifically, talk to your friends or family. Keeping their victim silent really is the key to an abuser's manipulation – whether that abuse is physical, sexual, mental or emotional. When someone is in that trapped state, they often do not even realise they are being abused, which allows them to continue to accept the situation and feel it is in part their fault. Talking allows the victim to articulate what is going on and work it through in their head, which in turn helps them to make sense of it. If you can't talk, then write it down, but share it with someone because a person on the outside will have a better perspective.

If you think you are already in an abusive relationship, or know someone that is, check out the signs with a little research on the web, searching terms like 'psychopath', 'narcissism' and 'toxic relationships'. I have detailed more of my own research as well as provided a resource page within my new book, *The Psychopath*. It's also possible to find help anonymously through various support groups – should you find it difficult to talk to someone close to you, speaking to someone from one of these groups might help.

Finally, don't hold on to the past. Life is too short to spend it looking back, so take whatever you can learn from any experience and use it to help you move forward. There is a lovely expression

I have heard, 'If you let it get you down, *you* go down.' So keep smiling and the future will be bright.

I wish you all the best, and I hope something wonderful happens to you today.

Regards,

Mary Turner Thomson

ACKNOWLEDGMENTS

I want to specifically thank all the amazing inspirational people I have spoken to in the course of writing this book, and who have all been victims themselves of this strange saga. These people have given me support, confidence, strength and hope again. They are the people who have talked to me at length and told me their stories, helping me to understand the full extent of the truth and allowing me to gain perspective. They made me realise I am by no means alone and gave me back my sense of self.

Thanks to Jenny Brown, my agent and new-found friend, who met me at an extremely stressful time in my life and has seen me make the transition back to normality.

Thanks also to my family and friends, particularly Carina and Mandy who have helped so enormously throughout and are the best friends you could wish to have. My family have also proved to be the best possible support in a crisis, and indeed every day. I would like to mention and thank for their help all the publishing staff for working so hard to actually put this book on the shelves. I also want to mention, and thank for their help and support throughout, Peter, Graham, Annie, Kate, Ben and my lovely Liz.

I would also like to acknowledge you, the reader, and say thank you for taking the time out of your extraordinary life to read my extraordinary story.

ABOUT THE AUTHOR

Photo © 2020 Mary Turner Thomson

Mary Turner Thomson grew up in Edinburgh. She has a BA Hons in Creative and Performing Arts, as well as diplomas in marketing, business advice and literature/creative writing. She worked as a business adviser, marketing consultant and motivational trainer before deciding to write a memoir of her marriage to a conman and bigamist.

Mary's forthcoming sequel to *The Bigamist*, *The Psychopath*, includes details about what Will Jordan has been doing since being deported, how her own family has moved forward, and what she now knows about psychopaths. Numerous new victims have come forward, new children have been discovered/born, and Mary even helped one victim set Will up in a police sting operation. If you want to find out more, sign up to Mary's website or follow her on Facebook and/or Twitter:

Website: **www.maryturnerthomson.com**

Facebook: **maryturnerthomson**

Twitter: **TheBigamistBook**

Mary is also the co-author of *Trading Places* (2009), the true story of how Natalie Hutchison suffered domestic abuse but took her life back by starting her own business, even winning the Trading Places award in 2006. She has also written a comedic book about what sociopaths say and what they *really* mean in *The Sociopath Subtext*.

Mary is currently working on her first novel, a psychological thriller.

If you liked this book, please leave a review on Amazon.